Your Fantasies May Be Hazardous to Your Health

Ligia Dantes has lectured widely in many countries, and has conducted hundreds of retreats, seminars, and workshops on the subjects of peace, responsibility, awareness, and human transformation. Born in Uruguay, she has traveled extensively in India and Nepal, and now lives in California.

About the Ligia Dantes Foundation

The Ligia Dantes Foundation was founded by Ligia in 1974 as the Self-Studies Institute. In 1984 she changed it to a non-profit, tax-exempt, educational organization.

The Foundation does not advocate the use of any spiritual practices or teachings resting solely on the authority of one individual. It does not engage in philosophical debates, psychotherapy, or esoteric practices. It is a place to address honestly, simply and directly the serious issues of life and to open oneself to true insight.

The Foundation operates the Woodhaven Retreat House, located in a tranquil country setting with beautiful gardens, where individuals come to share in the process of self-discovery through relaxation, meditation, peacefulness, and holistic living.

For more information please write to:

Ligia Dantes Foundation
P.O. Box 369
Nipomo, California 93444
U.S.A.

by the same author

The Unmanifest Self

Dearest Karen and Elise,

May you both be blessed with insight and compassion all your life. My love be with you always

Jim Santé

Your Fantasies May Be Hazardous to Your Health

HOW YOUR THOUGHTS CREATE YOUR WORLD

LIGIA DANTES

ELEMENT

Rockport, Massachusetts • Shaftesbury, Dorset
Brisbane, Queensland

© Ligia Dantes 1995

First published in the U.S.A. in 1995 by
Element Books, Inc.
PO Box 830, Rockport, MA 01966

Published in Great Britain in 1995 by
Element Books Limited
Shaftesbury, Dorset SP7 8BP

Published in Australia in 1995 by
Element Books Limited
for Jacaranda Wiley Limited
33 Park Road, Milton, Brisbane 4064

Cover design by the Bridgewater Book Company
Design by Roger Lightfoot
Typeset by Footnote Graphics, Warminster, Wiltshire
Printed and bound in the U.S.A.
by Edwards Bros. Inc.

British Library Cataloguing in Publication
data available

Library of Congress Cataloging in Publication Data
data available

ISBN 1–85230–687–4

Permission to reproduce the following copyright material
is gratefully acknowledged:
From *Tao Te Ching* by Lao Tsu, trans., English/Feng.
Copyright © 1972 by Gia-Fu Feng and Jane English.
Reprinted by permission of Alfred A. Knopf, Inc.
and Gower Publishing Limited.

Contents

To all my brothers and sisters in consciousness

ACKNOWLEDGMENTS

This book has been inspired by people from all over the world, and I am grateful to all of them. They are very beautiful, courageous individuals who dared inquire into the deepest recesses of their conditioning and beingness, honoring me with a trust to reflect their spiritual unfolding process.

I am also most grateful:

To Michael and Justine Toms for their encouraging and loving support of my work, making this book possible.

To Paul Cash for his sensibility in the handling of the publication of this book.

To Joanne Crandall for her unwavering loyalty, her loving care of my work and help with the syntax of these writings.

To Christine Cox for the sensitivity of her editing.

To Dr. Stuart Over, whose gift of a laptop computer made the writing of this book so much easier.

To Phil Gill for his inexhaustible support in all that was needed, and for formatting the manuscript.

Foreword

We live in times of great challenge and change. How do we maintain our balance in the midst of the turbulence? Most of us go around in a daze, though our minds fool us into thinking that we're fully conscious and aware. What Ligia has to say can help us, because her focus is on what is unchanging. She cuts through the illusion to the real—to what is. Ligia gives us a guide to penetrating the mental mist and opening the heart. She invites us to be spiritually mature, to venture beyond belief into another realm of knowing outside of time and space. This place is available to us in the here-and-now if we're willing to embrace the silence and listen. Ligia proves a useful map to this territory—but we have to make the journey.

I first met Ligia at a David Bohm "Dialogue" weekend in Ojai, California. Together with others we were exploring the possibilities of the "dialogue process" with the late physicist, who was its major proponent. On reflection now, it seems appropriate because, like Bohm, Ligia combines the rational with the ineffable in a compelling balance. Her approach returns us to ourselves and reminds us that we are the source, even as we may be seeking answers from outside.

The path Ligia points to demands the most from us. It is not easy, and is fraught with distractions. She provides the tools to help us see more clearly how our mind works, enabling us to expand our awareness and live more fully. She doesn't ask us to become a disciple, but rather to discover the way for ourselves. How refreshing!

Michael Toms
Ukiah, California

Michael Toms is an international radio interviewer and producer whose wide-ranging vision seeks to bring a transformation in consciousness to the whole of humanity.

1.

Preamble

"A spiritual evolved mind itself is happiness;
a deluded mind is suffering."—*Buddha*

For thousands of years gurus and teachers have talked about the "illusion" we human beings create. For most eastern religions, the world in which we are living is "Maya," a dream. To look at and question such statements is part of our responsibility if we are to experience our true nature, or as I refer to it, "Spiritupsychophysicalness." This word does not appear in any dictionary because it is this author's neologism. But it is appropriate as a description of our true nature.

Our nature is spiritual, psychic, and physical, *all at once*; therefore there are no dashes in my neologism to separate these three qualities of being. The word Spiritupsychophysicalness (you may complain that it is a little too long!) expresses the totality we are. This book approaches human beings from the standpoint of this totality, as it inquires into the normal thinking process of our organisms.

To feel ourselves as totally interrelated in the Universe and to be able to see "what is," to be devoid of fantasies, imaginings, cultural conditioning, knowledge, or beliefs, is a most freeing and glorious experience. It is truly a blessing, or "grace." *This is transcendence of ordinary consciousness.*

This transcendence occurs when we are willing to inquire

responsibly into our own way of functioning and our own conditioning. In other words, we must be *willing* to transcend. We must open the doors for this transcendence to take place.

Opening the doors means to inquire, to observe, to look at ourselves without judgment or evaluation. Observing and dialoging with hundreds of people in this way has taught me how the process of fantasy insidiously corrupts the innate intelligence of the thinking process in human beings. As a good friend said to me, "What is hard for me to see are the *assumption* fantasies, the *personal drama* fantasies, as well as the *normal projecting-of-the-future* fantasies. Fantasizing is a much more subtle and predominant process in our consciousness than we *think*." I totally agree! Much of the suffering in the world is brought about by the belief in the illusions that we, *without awareness*, have created. Images or fantasies truly shape our own little personal worlds, and our civilization!

Traveling abroad, and especially through India, brought me a deep feeling of love and compassion for the suffering we are enduring on our planet. I wanted to share with my brothers and sisters in the world my observations on all of the intricacies of imagination and fantasy, and the role they play in our daily living. I wanted to point out how our own image-making function is very helpful to our well-being, and how it also has become an insidiously deleterious process.

Furthermore, I wanted to share how wonderfully freeing it can be to awaken to the truth of our own nature.

These writings are based on observations and on actual contact with hundreds of people from all over the world. Thus this book is based on direct human experience, rather than acquired knowledge. Furthermore, the greatest emphasis is on the injurious aspects of fantasy, since there are already many instructive books on the positive aspects, especially on imagination and guided imagery for healing. I feel that the deleterious effects of fantasy have been neglected by many authors and purveyors of fantasy who promote it as a "fix-it-all," for self-improvement or for pleasure, without regard to possible detrimental consequences.

I want to affirm that whatever is discussed in
this book is not meant to propound a new theory
about fantasies or to convince anyone of a
particular point of view.

In order for the reader to be an active participant in this book, I propose that he/she embark upon a *direct* inquiry into its various proposals or statements. In other words, the reader will be responsible for his/her own discoveries; otherwise this will be just another book from which to absorb more learned, rather than directly experienced, knowledge.

I am not trying to derogate the accumulation of knowledge; but it is important to see that all the knowledge in the world has not brought peace of mind or healthy living to the majority of people, plants, and animals on the planet.

We are not totally aware of the danger we have created through our knowledge. By this I mean that our inventions (such as nuclear weapons) were, at one time, simply an image or fantasy in someone's mind, based on accumulated knowledge. Particularly through technological knowledge, we have damaged ourselves—in some areas irremediably.

In his book *Kindness, Clarity and Insight* the Dalai Lama writes: "It is said that with the help of wisdom, compassion can become limitless." It is of the utmost importance that we experience limitless compassion for all creatures of the earth and that we protect the planet; therefore, we must use our intelligence with *wisdom*.

It is for this reason that this book is written in a simple, commonsense manner, as a challenge to the intellectually adept as well as for the experientially oriented person. The challenge is to depend on our natural human wisdom (insights) rather than on acquired concepts and repetitions of learned explanations.

Within these written pages, you and I will do the inquiring together in invisible, interrelated ways, even though we appear to be separate. Of course, I cannot offer proof of this interrelationship anymore than I can prove the non-solid (the constant atomic particle exchange) nature of matter, such as wood.

In the same manner that we see the wood superficially as solid, we see ourselves superficially as separate entities. Even though quantum physics and religion have given us many theories about out interconnectedness, we still must rely on our intuition and insight for the true *experience* of Oneness. We do not have sophisticated equipment to prove it.

It is my intention to bring to our awareness the *need*, as well as the *possibility*, of transcending ordinary consciousness. We need to awaken from our somnolence, not only to experience well-being, but also for our own survival and that of the planet.

This book, my friend, is about you and me, humanity and the planet.

2.

Introduction to the Exploration of Fantasy

In our present times the use of imagination has proliferated through human consciousness as fast as fire spreading through dry California brush. Everywhere we see the wide use of imagination—fantasy—from the entertainment world, commerce, education, film, and television, to workshops on healing.

More recently, in the area of healing, physicians have proved that humans can use their imagination to improve their psychophysical health. Drs. Carl Simonton, Larry LeShan, Dean Ornish, and Larry Dossey, as well as many other physicians are advocating the use of imagination combined with psychotherapy, medical care, prayer, diet, and lifestyle changes. Their main focus has been with patients suffering from heart conditions, cancer, and emotional problems. They use imagery as an important tool in the healing process and for increasing the efficiency of the immune systems of their patients.

Imagination and fantasy have become very important tools in our civilization. Using one's imagination is encouraged in schools, in the arts, in the work place, and even in relationships. In the fields of entertainment and fashion, fantasy is the basic force bringing millions of dollars to these industries.

Projects such as space travel and the building of a space station are based on the imagination of professionals with visions. By the same token, the atom bomb was once a fantasy, an image in the minds of physicists. This fantasy has evolved into the manifestation of atomic weaponry. This kind of imagination is of great danger to the planet and its inhabitants. In later chapters we will inquire more deeply into the relationship of imagination and survival at the personal and global levels.

Imagination, fantasy, and hallucinations are "occurrences" within the thinking function. They are all different aspects of the thinking process of the human body/mind. Imagination and fantasy are considered normal aspects of thinking, while hallucinations are considered pathological. However, I would like to contend that imagination and fantasy—when used in a particular way, as they are in our civilization, and especially when used for profit—may be deleterious, dangerous processes leaning towards the pathological.

The most obvious use of fantasy for profit, with attendant danger, is in the film industry. Film violence has become more and more explicit and gory, showing the audiences more and more "inventive" ways to maim and kill people, and destroy the planet.

In the area of sex, fantasy has proliferated into a large pornographic industry—magazines, films, and videos further enticing the imagination of consumers at the high cost of human degradation and the exploitation of children, women, and men.

Perhaps the most pernicious fantasies, those which bring great pain and conflict to the individual, are related to the self-image. In our daily living we may carry concerns about how we appear to others, what they think of us, or how we are performing on our jobs—all bringing feelings of inadequacy. These concerns may raise the level of anxiety to such extremes that the body is injured (ulcers, hypertension, colitis, etc.). Tension changes the chemistry of the body and reduces the effectiveness of the immune system.

Daydreaming, another common form of fantasizing, is a well-accepted, normal way of functioning, and very little attention is given to the danger it brings. Daydreams are fantasies that take away our energy, distract us from our tasks, and often endanger us on the job or on the highways.

Perhaps the unhealthy use of fantasy is disguised so well,

behind the notion of imagination and creativity, that we cannot see the forest for the trees. It is suggested here, firstly, that it is imperative to question established patterns in our societies that are based on imagination; secondly, that we begin to discern what is helpful and what is injurious in what we call imagination and creativity.

Imagination is a powerful human quality and a most useful tool when applied with wisdom. However, when it is an unconscious, or conscious but *unaware* process of fantasy, it is greatly destructive, keeping humanity in vicious circles of illusions.

By *unaware*, I mean that people may be *cognizant* (conscious) of the fantasies in their minds, but oblivious to the consequences of these fantasies in their psychophysical structures. For example, chain smokers may be cognizant of the dangers of tobacco but continue their habit, ignoring the physical symptoms and the precariousness of their state of health. The difference between being *cognizant* and having *total awareness* will become clearer as we begin to examine these terms and their relationship to fantasy.

Imagining and fantasizing are normal activities of the body/mind. Therefore, to understand how destructive or beneficial they may be to the human organism and to society, it is important that we begin giving special attention to our psychophysical way of functioning. Furthermore, we need to investigate how cultural conditioning perpetuates fantasies that are detrimental to the entire planet.

I feel we are responsible for our own well-being as much as we are responsible for the well-being of humanity and the planet. As a matter of fact, fantasy may keep us from personal growth and spiritual unfolding without us being aware, because it hides the perniciousness of certain repetitive patterns of consciousness at large. This occurs because human beings are unaware of the destructive forces within the great movements of consciousness at the individual and social levels.

Let us begin the investigation of what imagination and fantasy are, how they may be used constructively and effectively, and how they may be destroying you and the rest of humanity.

3.

A Look at the Meaning of Fantasy

The word *fantasy* has some derogatory connotations, especially when used as a description of an adult's state of mind considered unrealistic—that is, *unreal* according to what *we view by agreement* to be *real*.

Let me exemplify what I mean by "real by agreement."

We base our correct time on an *agreed-upon* imaginary line going through Greenwich, England (a meridian which, in our minds, divides the world into time zones). The dictionary tells us that "the official time for most of the world is Greenwich Time"; that is, "the *mean solar time*" of the meridian at Greenwich.

Time is very important to us. For example, we do not dare disbelieve this agreed-upon reality when we have to board a plane. If a person were to proclaim, "There is no such thing as time" (which may be true) and argue with the airline employees to postpone takeoff until he/she arrives at the airport, that person would be considered mentally unbalanced or neurotic, living in a world of fantasy.

Through knowledge we learn that a mountain is a section of the earth rising up high above the sea level—not just a few feet, but a certain relative measurement which we invented and agree to be true. If we call a molehill a mountain (or vice versa) we are "unrealistic."

We consider an unrealistic person a dreamer, or maybe

neurotic, not totally normal; or as it is commonly said, "He is not all there," or "She lives in a fantasy world."

Therefore, to examine carefully the basic meaning of fantasy from a direct, simple, and very commonsense point of view, it is important to explore what *we have agreed* to call *fantasy*. The best way to begin is to look at dictionary definitions of this word. According to Webster's New International Dictionary of the English Language (second edition, 1954),

FANTASY means:

- "Act or function of forming images or representations, whether in direct perception or in memory; also an image or impression derived through sensation;"
- "capricious or erratic fancy;"
- "hallucination; phantom; apparition;"
- "desire; inclination;"
- "an imagined fulfillment of desire, as in daydreaming;"
- "a chimerical or fantastical notion, from any source."

And according to Websters New World Dictionary of the American Language (second edition, 1968),

TO FANTASIZE means:

- "To create or imagine in a fantasy; have daydreams about;"
- "to indulge in reverie;"
- "to create or develop imaginative and often fantastic views or ideas;"
- "to portray in the mind."

We also need to see how *imagination* is defined.

IMAGINATION means:

- "Power or faculty of the mind by which it conceives and forms ideas of things from knowledge communicated by the organs of the senses;"
- "the faculty by which we can bring absent objects and perceptions forcibly before the mind;"
- "the constructive or creative faculty."

TO IMAGINE means:

* "To bring to the mind's eye; to conceive in thought;"
* "to think; to skim or devise; to suppose; to fancy;"
* "to form a mental picture of something that is not there."

The first three words defining "fantasy" are *act or function*. This refers to the natural act or function of the human organism (body/mind), the ability we possess to think, to make images or representations—ideas.

A child, in order to learn what things are, must have a functional apparatus for learning; that is, an able body/mind. For a child to learn what a tree is, she/he must first have a brain *able* to have a representation, an image or idea of the object perceived. Secondly, the object must be pointed out and named "tree" by someone else. Furthermore, there has to be an ability in the organism to retain that image (memory) so that the object can later be recognized as tree.

If humans did not possess organs (like the brain) with an innate thinking ability function, a memory function, and an ability to imagine as well as to express the images or ideational process in words, we could not have art or religion, nor would we be able to dialogue about them. Furthermore, we would not have the kind of civilization we presently have.

Let us continue with the latter part of the first dictionary definition of fantasy:

> a) (act or function of) "forming images or representations *whether in direct perception or in memory*"[emphasis is the author's]: b) "image or impression *derived through sensation.*"

Attention to this part of the definition is of the utmost importance, for it provides a significant clue to our way of functioning. It is apparent that whether we perceive something directly (an impression derived through the senses) or have a memory of something, it is all imagery. In other words, whether it is direct perception or memory, it is all *representation in mind*. This means that from this particular point of view, one may say that every image, every idea, every thought formed by the mind function is actually fantasy, *regardless of the origin of the stimuli.*

Could the thought process be only fantasy?

In Webster's dictionary, the meaning of the verb *to imagine* confirms this suspicion. To imagine means: "to *conceive in thought, to think; to form a mental picture.*"

To *think* is to make images, and to *fantasize* is also to make images. Then, to fantasize is to *think!*

Try this experiment:

Notice this book in front of you. The *thought* or the image of the book in your mind, *in this very moment,* is not the book itself, right? Therefore, the book in the mind is the representation of the object being perceived through the senses; it is a thought, a mental picture, an image of the book perceived. Next, close your eyes and remember the book. Set aside the book and remember what happened to you yesterday morning. You are now also having images or pictures in your mind. You are thinking, right?

Now try another experiment. Imagine sucking on a piece of lemon. Just the *idea* of tasting a lemon can bring a physical reaction as if you were tasting an actual lemon. Your lips may pucker or your mouth salivate, whether it is a fantasy or a direct perception.

Through these kinds of experiments you may be able to recognize that whether you are seeing an object or remembering a past incident, a similar *mind/body process* of thought is involved. The difference is in the stimulus. One is an object (outside stimulus), the other is a memory (inner stimulus).

Stating that "the thought process is *only* fantasy" may raise some eyebrows. However, if we examine very closely the nature of the thinking process in ourselves, we can see that regardless of the kind of content in mind, the thinking function remains the same. Therefore, this process will produce:

- the image of an outer object we perceive through any of our senses;
- the mental pictures of memories (short term or long past);

- the imagination of the future;
- the image of a religious experience, or of insights;
- the creative image of music and other art forms.

All of these are within the *content* of thought (ideas, images, representations). Regardless of the kind or quality of the mind's content, it remains a fantasy from the point of view of the action or function of the organism—the image maker. In other words, as far as the production of images is concerned, the image maker does not distinguish between stimuli; it just makes images. Whether they are sensations, perception of an object, a memory of an incident or emotions, a religious experience, or an insight, stimuli become representations, images in the mind. This is cognizance.

> *In the brain* per se, *there seems to be no distinction between the reality of the images. To the image maker, one image is just as real as the next.*
>
> *Please observe yourself to see if this is true in your own experience. A helpful experiment may be to look alternately at objects in front of you and at memories. First you look at an object. Be aware of that image. Then close your eyes and remember something that happened yesterday.*

Assuming that thought as a representation is fantasy (you have to see for yourself), we can then ask: What *kind* of thinking have we agreed is fantasy? We have gone through a detailed examination of the first meaning of fantasy. Now we want to approach the other connotations which will give us a more complete meaning of the word.

The second dictionary meaning is:

- "capricious or erratic fancy," together with
- "hallucination, phantom, apparition;"
- "an imagined fulfillment of desire as in daydream;"
- "a chimerical or fantastical notion from any source."

All of these are the common meanings we use to refer to fantasy, and they carry a sense of derogation. Initially, we want to discern between the first and the second set of meanings. We have established that the first meaning refers to the natural act or function of mind/body of "forming images or representations, whether in direct perception derived through the senses, through insights, or from memory."

All the other definitions of the word fantasy—fancy, daydream, chimerical notion, etc.—refer to the *content*, and more specifically to the *kind* of representation. In general, according to the dictionary, these definitions (fancy, daydream, hallucination, apparition, and chimera) are all images created in the mind but with no *concrete* or *objective* reality. Thus fantasy in this context refers to images not based on sensorial object perception.

Indeed, in the general usage of the word, to fantasize or hallucinate is to think or see something that is not there. This close examination of the different meanings of fantasy will become more helpful and clear as we continue to look deeply into our thinking process. In the following chapters we will take a closer look at the *contents* of fantasy and its consequences, both beneficial and detrimental.

Summary

Let me reiterate that we are considering fantasy:
- first, as a natural part of the thinking process (images) of human organisms;
- second, as *representations* in mind *different* from those representations considered to be perceived from the objective world, our reality, or our *agreed upon reality*;
- third, as a conditioned process (habitual way of thinking influenced by the acculturation process); and
- fourth, as a process whose contents may be beneficial (as in the use of imagination for the healing process) and as a process that may have detrimental consequences in our bodies, in our way of living, and on the planet.

We are not looking at fantasy with any judgment or evaluation. We are neutrally observing a natural, human function. (By neutrally I mean without trying to change, criticize, or praise.)

> *Please take a moment to experience directly the words in these writings. They can only be meaningful when you discover, through your own personal exploration, the truth of your own way of functioning.*
>
> *A neutral attitude is imperative.*

Our ability to think has been analyzed, hypothesized, and explained ad infinitum. But do we, by ourselves, truly know the workings of our own thinking process in the moment of life itself?

Can we observe, objectively, our own thinking process in the very instant it occurs? Can we experience thinking without thought?

> *The challenge here is to stop reading this book for a moment and look for yourself, to question and see what the above statements mean. Are you able to do this? Or will you continue to read, looking for further clues as to how to do this? ... Well?*
>
> *Of course, this exercise reveals a different approach to this book. I have requested at the beginning that you neither believe nor disbelieve what I am proposing.*
>
> *Well, this is it! This is the challenge!*
>
> *It is your participation in the process, in the moment of now, that makes this book an alive action, a truly different approach. If it is read*

*merely for more accumulation of knowledge, this
book may be as useless as millions of books
already written.*

**My friend, YOU are the one who makes the
difference!**

4.

The Thought Process

In the previous chapter I suggested that all thought is fantasy in that it is never other than a representation, either of an object (outer stimulus coming through the senses) or a memory (inner stimulus) or an insight (inner/outer stimulus). This brings up some questions: If all is fantasy, is anything real? Is it all maya, illusion? What is reality and what is fantasy in the thought process?

The thought of an object is ordinarily not considered fantasy, but *reality*. However, the memories attached to the object are considered *non-reality*. For example: If I perceive a rose, it is *reality*; but my associations to the rose, such as imagining a gardener who takes care of it or my annoyance with him for not having it well watered, is *non-reality*.

This is how we *separate* what we call *real thought* from *fantasy*. The thought of an object is considered "realistic thinking," but the fantasy is considered "unrealistic thinking."

We are very certain of what our own senses perceive. Generally, we believe what we see with our eyes, even though it may be an optical illusion. The ever-popular example is that of the man in the desert seeing an oasis. Often we see water at a distance on a highway, only to find out that what we saw was not "real." After a recent earthquake in California, a police car fell several feet onto a broken part of a freeway. The policeman's eyes saw a continuous cement road although it was, in fact, broken. There were no other senses to tell him differently; therefore he could believe only the information given by his eyes. Regardless of the countless times we are bamboozled, tricked by our senses, we continue to fully trust in them as our primary—and sometimes only—revealers of reality.

Memory may also be considered *real* (accurate, a fact) or *unreal* (fantasy) depending on the circumstance. Especially in a court of law, memory may be considered fact or fiction depending on who is remembering (a child, a person with credibility, a person of ill repute, etc.) or who is judging or interpreting the memory (an objective person such as a judge or a skeptic, or someone with a hidden agenda). Nevertheless, to the person experiencing, memory is always real, true.

We like to think we agree on what is reality and what is fantasy. However, let us question popular beliefs by investigating for ourselves, directly, what is real and what is fantasy *for us*, in our daily living.

> *It is up to you to be at observation of your own*
> *beliefs about reality and fantasy. When is*
> *thought a reality to you and when is it fantasy?*

It will be useful here to notice that *to think* about thought is actually more thinking. To *be at observation* of thought is a different process which we need to understand.

The expression "be at observation" is used here as synonymous with *have insight or full awareness*. That is, we want to be able to experience deeply and holistically what thought is. However, we want to derive this deep understanding without intellectual analysis based solely on psychological knowledge, philosophical views, or religious dogma.

This may at first appear impossible; however, we can put our knowledge to one side by not referring to it whenever we want an explanation. This will facilitate a dependence on our intuition. Furthermore, if we were to give up all of what we have learned in order to enter into direct inquiry, we would be left in a state of mind tantamount to a "tabula rasa" state (a clear slate). I mean that by giving up, we would no longer believe in learned knowledge as the only truth. This would provide an opportunity for something new, an unknown, a *full awareness* to take place. I do not mean a new thought, but the possibility of a revolution in our own way of knowing, brought about by *insight*.

Please notice that in these writings, *full awareness* is differentiated from *thought* or *cognition*. This differentiation is important in further understanding fantasy.

We are using *awareness* in the sense of an alertness that is not present in simple cognizance.

For example, one can be cognizant (knowledgeable, informed) of the danger of driving too fast but not be *aware* or *alert* to the totality of the consequences at the moment of action. A driver may be cognizant of a stop sign at a certain location but at a given moment will miss it. The person is not purposely ignoring it, but is so involved in something else—perhaps listening to the radio or worrying about a problem—that he/she goes right on through the stop sign without awareness of its existence. The person is definitely conscious, cognizant, but unaware of all that is going on at that moment.

Awareness is the alertness of an animal in the jungle, where all is included in the very moment of now. In full awareness there is no dwelling on anything other than "what is."

In this book we will use the words *full awareness, insight*, and *being at observation* as representations of experiences occurring *beyond* the thought process; in other words, as a different dimension of consciousness. Experiences of this state are often very difficult to describe and sometimes hardly recognizable in consciousness. Nevertheless, they carry the power and speed of lightning and are, at times, life transforming.

Insight is like the electrical discharge during a storm. The thinking produced by the insight is like the thunder following the lightning. Thus, even though we experience thinking associated with insight, the thought process is only the subsequent reverberation in the mind of this extraordinary and powerful phenomenon.

If fantasy is thought, and full awareness is beyond thought, it follows that fantasy is not full awareness. If, therefore, while we look at fantasy we *see* with *awareness* the thought process as well as the content, this event would be experienced from a different dimension of consciousness.

Let me emphasize that to merely look at something it is not necessarily to *see* it; it is like looking at your watch and not seeing the time. When we *look*, we direct our attention towards something, but we actually see it when *insight* or full awareness unfolds in our consciousness. If there is a distraction of some kind while we are directing our inquiry and fo
specific object, we are "looking" but may not n
with wisdom. Looking without seeing is no mo
lectual exercise.

We need to discern how our own thinking fu
intelligent and beneficial, enlivened by *awarene*
process of unaware conditioned thinking, day
fantastical notions, having deleterious consequer
sciousness and therefore in our way of living.

- Thinking enlivened with awareness is *clear* thi
  very different from automatic, conditioned thii
- Clear thinking is spontaneous and wise. Con
  ing is a repetition of acquired conditioning.
- Clear thinking is on "what is." Conditioned th
  on memory and may give rise to fantasy!

We need to be aware of our general beliefs about fa
same time keep in mind that, as representation, there
or differentiation between thoughts of objects and th
associations, memories, or fantasies (such as fancy, da
tion, hallucination, chimera).

In other words, within the thinking process everything is image or representation.

5.

Daydreaming and its Consequences

Because daydreaming is the most commonly accepted form of fantasy, it will serve well as the starting point for an exploration of this insidious and pervasive form of thinking.

Daydream is defined in Webster's New World Dictionary of the American Language (second edition) as "a pleasant dream-like thinking or wishing; reverie; a pleasing but visionary notion or scheme."

Young children are good models for observing daydreaming in action. Their thought processes are constantly active, elaborating stories about their toys or objects they come across. Daydreaming is a very natural process in human beings from the very beginning of the cognitive process. But to what extent does this natural process of childhood become habitual? What are the consequences of habitual daydreaming?

Let me give you some simple examples from the many cases I have witnessed.

We had a secretary who, from time to time, would stare into space or out through a window. She would sit motionless for several minutes, unaware that I was observing her. At times her face was practically blank, and occasionally a frown would appear on her forehead; at other times she seemed to be in conversation with someone. When I asked if she was all right, she would say with embarrassment, "Oh I was just thinking! My family ... you know." She finally had to leave her job, agreeing that she needed to go through some kind of psychotherapy or counseling. Her daydreaming had become more important to her than her employment.

A different type of case is that of Jack, a retired carpenter residing in the city. He is overweight and his health is precarious.

He is planning to have a farm. We find him talking to his neighbor, enthusiastically and meticulously explaining the way he plans to work the land. He elaborates on the specific kind of tractors he will have to use, the kinds of cows and the number of chickens he wants to raise.

Jack brings out a magazine dedicated to farming, and proudly shows his neighbor some beautiful pictures of farm lands, tractors and award winning "Jerseys." They both become engrossed in the daydream of farming, practically smelling the hay. Jack has found a new friend and a partner for his fantasy world, because his neighbor is a fan of country living and wishes he could move to a farm himself.

As a young boy, Jack was supported in his daydreaming by his mother who would sit and listen to him, believing he would really be a farmer some day. Jack was very convincing in his stories and his knowledge enhanced the possibilities for the fantasy to come true.

Jack never became a farmer. He is now ninety years old, and he will occasionally say with a tone of sadness and pride, "If I could have had a farm, I would have been the best doggoned farmer in Mississippi!" adding, "and I would have been successful too, because I did my homework!"

Does this story sound typical to you?

Cases like these repeat themselves a thousandfold every day all over the planet. Such domination by fantasy is part of our conditioned way of thinking that is encouraged and maintained by various aspects of the society around us.

In the case of Jack, we see a habitual "daydreamer" encouraged first by his mother and now by a neighbor with a similar dream. Furthermore, the magazines on the subject of farming are filled with advertisements that glamorize the products and the circumstances of farm living. Jack had a "heap" of support from family, friends, and society's conditioning! His case is an example of typical habitual daydreaming that goes on for a lifetime. But it does not need to go on forever. There are people who become *aware* of their conditioned habitual thinking patterns and stop.

Let me relate another case where, in contrast to the previous two, the person has an insight that changes his way of living.

Norman was a teacher at a college. He was forty-two years old, married with two children. He enjoyed teaching. He was interested in Eastern philosophy and self-understanding. His relationship with his family was good, and in general he was well adjusted and content. But he regretted not having enough money to get a sailboat. In his youth he had loved sailing, and had spent much of his free time at the library learning about boats, sailing, the weather, and everything relating to nautical living. He read hundreds of magazines over the years, and had pictures of the greatest sailing boats in the world's history. He delighted in going sailing and talking to friends who had sailboats docked at marinas. Now, however, he had very little time for all this, and each day he regretted more and more not being able to have a sailboat. He kept looking at magazines and daydreaming of having a boat some day.

Norman was also very interested in knowing himself. He had taken courses on meditation and self-improvement, and workshops on "How to make your dreams a reality." These workshops had been a disappointment to him because at forty-two he still did not have his coveted sailboat. Nothing had helped him to achieve his dream. However, he continued to observe himself to the best of his ability and persevered in his quest for truth—meditating, reading books on psychology, religion, and Eastern philosophy.

One day Norman found a picture of the dream of his life, *the* perfect sailboat, in a magazine. It was there right in front of him. It was beautiful, with all the best features he could have ever imagined. He was so excited about it that he began to daydream of being in the middle of the ocean on this magnificent sailing ship. He began to experience vividly the wind in his face, the exhilaration of the sound of the bow cutting through the waters, the rush of shifting the position of the jib. Turning to his imaginary sailing partner he said, almost shouting aloud, "Coming about!" ... and suddenly he *saw* himself clearly.

There was no boat, no sails, no water, no wind. All there was in front of him was a picture of a specific kind of boat.

He was *aware of the moment of now*, just as it is!

He experienced himself totally as a human being, deriving great enjoyment from looking at a picture of a sailboat in a magazine! There were no judgments or evaluations. "I do not want a sailboat; I want to read and fantasize about it!" Norman realized.

It is all so clear! He is living the truth of the moment.

He realized that all the years of resentment about not having a boat masked his enjoyment in fantasizing. "It is more fun to fantasize about it than to go through the trouble of working harder to get the damn thing," said Norman to himself, with a smile on his face and a great sense of relief. "I don't have to resent not having a boat ... this is crazy! I just *thought* I wanted a boat."

And he further realized, "If I tell the truth, I am free of resentment" ... and the wonderful adage came to his mind, "YEA! THE TRUTH WILL SET YOU FREE!" He laughed as he experienced a great sense of well-being that he had never experienced before.

Norman is now forty-eight years old. He has begun a new career in politics. He is campaigning for a school board position and is very involved in community services for the youth of his country. He rarely looks at sailing magazines, and thoroughly enjoys taking orphaned children on sailing trips. A couple, who are friends of Norman, often make their boat available for these events.

He is sailing more now than he was before and has stopped resenting not owning a sailboat. He continues to be observant of himself and is using meditation techniques on a daily basis for relaxation and awareness.

Norman's story illustrates a true moment of *insight*.

In that moment there is awareness of thought *as thought*; it is recognized as fantasy, as *unrealistic thinking*. The fantasy content is no longer believed to be real. In this kind of *neutral* experience, while the thinking process is at the peak of an emotional reverie, a sudden and inexplicable, non-judgmental clarity about what is actually happening occurs, and Norman is a new man.

Awareness or insights usually affect our way of thinking for a lifetime, and often are followed by radical change in our way of living. Unfortunately, we do not have a prescription or a technique to produce these unexpected blessings. However, we can be observant, as much as possible, of our own way of functioning, for this seems to open doors to such extraordinary blessed moments.

It is of interest to notice that in Jack's case, there is no curiosity about himself. He is like an automaton, a thinking machine entrapped in its own circuits. It is as though something stopped growing, or what I call unfolding, as a total human being in the universe. This is not to say that it is bad to be like Jack. He is a typical example of our own somnolent consciousness, and it is important to find out to what extent we also are entrapped in our own circuits of conditioned thinking. Norman was tangled in his fantasy about owning a sailboat and also in the fantasy of resenting that he did not. In his case, the brooding was also part of the complexity of the boat fantasy.

The thought process affects the entire organism. It is not an isolated process somewhere in a nebulous world we call mind. The problem resides in the seeming reality of feelings, sensations, and emotions we experience that allows us to *believe* our own fantasies, blinding us to the truth of the moment of *now*.

Jack is totally convinced he will have that farm; each time he talks about his dream farm he is totally involved, heart and soul. All the appropriate emotions, sensations, and feelings about having the farm are there in full, real force. The habitual thinking reinforces the belief in the fantasy. The more he thinks about it, the more he believes in it. It is a vicious circle. Unlike

Jack, Norman has the facility of curiosity and, perhaps, a passion for truth. Without this, would he have been open to insight? Probably not!

I suggest that a passion for truth and an intense curiosity about existence are most important ingredients in the process of complete human unfolding. It has been my observation that people engrossed in their fantasies as Jack was—or constantly daydreaming about their goals without regard for anyone else, or engrossed in their daydream-worries, or involved in the fantasies of soap operas—all remain at the same dimension of consciousness, with no further unfolding awareness throughout their lives.

Daydreaming is a powerful and yet debilitating way of thinking. It takes the great power of insight or awareness to actually stop it.

> *Are you a "daydreamer"? Do you justify it with*
> *the thought, "Everybody is!" or do you tell*
> *yourself, "I have to have a dream of something*
> *better or I will never improve myself?"*

I have heard comments from hundreds of people who are convinced of the *need* to have a dream in life and are trying very hard to *make it*. But no matter what they do, they are not able to attain it. They spend thousands of dollars in a myriad of workshops learning how to go about fulfilling the dream. They are frustrated and unhappy, but unwilling to give up their dream. Needless to say, they never examine their fantasy process. Norman was lucky to be in a process of unfolding awareness, which he honored by his continuous observation of himself.

One of the most common and dangerous times for daydreaming is while driving a vehicle. Perhaps most accidents happen as a consequence of the unawareness of our state of mind. Of course we say that we were "just thinking," not fantasizing, when we just miss hitting someone, or another car. This is a hazardous form of thinking! For any violation we commit or dangerous situation we put ourselves in, we may use a justification such as, "I was so worried about my family ..." or "I was so upset with my boss."

Are you familiar with this kind of reasoning?
You may recall many other justifications you
have heard or learned.

Fantasy or daydreaming is responsible for industrial accidents as well. Many workers have suffered serious accidents while bitterly fantasizing about their dispute with their boss, or imagining how much happier they would be if they "were in a different kind of a job." Daydreaming, fantasizing, is a mental activity that slows down the productivity in many areas of the workplace and puts people at risk.

Daydreaming is great for children.
Daydreaming in adults is infantile thinking.
After a certain age, daydreaming, fantasy, is not intelligent thinking.
Daydreaming can fulfill desire and block action. It takes away interest in others, making relationships difficult. It aids in perpetuating a self-centered consciousness.

This is not a criticism, it is simply a fact. It is damaging for us as adults to daydream and *we are not aware of it!*

Of course, there are the Martin Luther Kings who have *a dream* and incite people to fulfill that dream by *acting now*. But I wonder how many people actually act now, and how many just stay within the dream?

I would like to differentiate between having a vision, an actual goal (you may call it a dream) where you are actively doing something towards it every day, and the dream that is only a fancy (daydream) that fulfills desire but has no action. A true vision, an actual goal, always involves what is present as well as what is to be in the future. There is no thought of "maybe someday." There is no rigidity; plans are changed as needed according to unfolding circumstances in any actions towards the goal. Contrary to this, a daydream, a fancy, is stagnant; the content of the dream is *always the same*. The only purpose is to achieve the fulfillment of a mental desire by mental action—thoughts—not by physical accomplishment. Expressions such as "someday ..." are copious and constant in the reveries. Visions or actual goals are healthy and invigorating. Daydreams, fancies, are infantile, paralyzing, and unhealthy.

This may sound very negative to you. And of course, as we show later, having good, positive daydreaming may be beneficial to the mind/body. After all, "Good thoughts," says Dr. Deepak Chopra, "bring about endorphins, which help the immune system." While that is a fact, it does not always work that way with habitual daydreaming.

Thought is electrical energy, chemistry, body activity of which we are not conscious. We are barely cognizant of the consequences of the thinking process in the whole body. Let's say you had a bitter disagreement with a co-worker and you felt belittled. Now you are driving home from work and you are fantasizing about telling that person how angry you are, and it goes something like this:

"You have the nerve to tell me that I am a slow worker? I may be slow because I am detailed, because I care and take pride in my work!" ... and you watch the face of your co-worker in your scenario react ... and then go on. "But you, you just go faster because you have to make up for all the cigarette breaks you take during the day!" ...

At that moment someone cuts in front of your car and you go into a rage. "You fumbling idiot! Where do you think you are going? I hope a policeman saw you! I hope you get a big fat ticket! Jeez ... !!!"

You are now more rattled, but soon you go back to your fantasy. "Another moron like you in the world ..." you tell your co-worker in your imagination, as if the *moment of now* were part of the fantasy. And the reverie picks up where it was interrupted and goes on and on, over and over again as you tell that person, *now*, all of what you feel you should have said but did not have the courage to say *then*.

By the time you get home you are really exhausted from

having worked all day under tension. To compound your fatigue, the memories of what happened at work and your fantasies about it have brought about more tension in your muscles, and more injurious emotional chemistry, such as acidic gastric juices in your empty stomach. You have a headache and feel nauseous. You are still angry and suffering from the effects of the tensions in your whole body.

Most of the time people do not consider the physical strain, but are concerned with the psychological upheaval. So they try to get help.

The usual advice from a friend or a psychotherapist, is, "Do not leave a situation until you have completed whatever you have to say." "Speak up! Complete your communications! Assert yourself!", and so on. Or you might be advised to look into your past and find out what it is that stops you from speaking up in difficult situations. So you go to a counselor for psychotherapy and find out.

Now, having done this, you actually know what causes you to freeze up or be intimidated by others, particularly authority figures; but you still have a hard time saying *all* you want to say in a moment of frustration or anger. So you still fantasize about your predicament and try to resolve your discomforts through a conditioned, imaginary mode.

How about simply becoming *aware* of what is happening to you at the *very moment of fantasy*? Can you *see* or *be at observation* of the fantasy *as* fantasy?

> *At the moment of fantasy, can you experience*
> *that the only reality is in the sensations,*
> *feelings, emotions, and images (thought) in the*
> *mind/body? Can you experience the deleterious*
> *consequences of the mind's activity in the rest of*
> *the body when the emotions are strong enough*
> *to make you very tense or overly excited? Can*
> *you be aware of what you are actually doing at*
> *the very moment of now? Remember that we are*
> *not talking about cognition, but rather*

awareness in the moment of life itself. It is up to
you to answer these questions for yourself. You
are the only one responsible for your own
unfolding!

Remember Norman? He was satisfying his desire through fantasy, but continued to resent not having a boat. He was unaware that his resentment and the pleasure of the fantasy masked the truth that he did not want to buy a boat. He realized that what he really wanted to do was to fantasize and *not take action*.

It is very important to observe how much energy is spent on daydreaming about something for which no action is possible at the moment of fantasy itself. Whether you are a secretary, a housewife, a teacher, a student, an industrial worker, a preacher, or an executive, you have an opportunity to observe how often any form of daydreaming happens to you.

Furthermore, you can discover to what extent fantasy or daydreaming may:

- increase disagreements and mistakes;
- erode relationships;
- slow down productivity; and
- increase the danger of accidents.

Being in the present is the constructive way of thinking; that is mindfulness! Being mindful means attending to every thing we are doing right now. It is doing what we are doing, not thinking one thing and doing another.

When we live mindfully we are in harmony. Our bodies are more relaxed and therefore healthier; our minds are clearer and understand more deeply; and our hearts are joyful because we care for everyone rather than just ourselves. This is living in the integrity of wholeness; it is living a spiritual life.

Living "what is" rather than daydreaming is one of the greatest gifts we can give to ourselves. When daydreaming ends, life begins.

The most important points to observe are:

a) that we may not be aware to what extent what we call "just thinking" is actually daydreaming;
b) that most of our waking life may be spent daydreaming;
c) that we are not always aware of how real some of our fantasies are to us, to the extent that our whole body reacts as if they were actually happening;
d) that daydreaming may be detrimental to our health and relationships; and
e) that when we daydream we are not living in the *now* and therefore *we miss the preciousness of the moment of life itself.*

The remedy for daydreaming is mindfulness. In mindfulness we attend to the activity in the moment of now, bringing every action to the fullest possible completion. In mindfulness we are absorbed each moment in the activity and all that is happening in our surroundings at the same time. There is no preoccupation with self-image. "Am I doing this right so that I don't look like a fool?" This kind of question would not arise in a moment of mindfulness. "I wish I could have been a ballerina!" and a consequent fantasy would not enter consciousness. It is easy and very beneficial to practice mindfulness.

You might try being observant while you are driving a car. If your mind wanders into a fantasy, gently bring your attention back to the action "driving the car"; look at the scenery; see how much farther your eyes are actually perceiving. You might become aware of what you were missing around you before.

You can apply this practice to any activity in your everyday life. Daily meditation is a most helpful practice of mindfulness, when meditation has no particular objective than just being. However, there may be other techniques, that have different goals that may be of benefit. It is up to the individual to find the process that is most appropriate for his or her unfolding.

6.

Self-image: Reality or Fantasy?

Self-image is very meaningful to human beings; it is also a source of suffering.

We humans, and perhaps to some extent other animals, are self-aware. To have an image of oneself is part of our natural functioning.

We are cognizant of our own bodies and protect them; doing so is instinctual in us. The ability to be aware of ourselves as independent or separate from others and the environment is supported by all of our senses.

Our eyes, ears, nose, skin, and taste buds are important survival receptors of our organisms. They contribute to our experience of being a unit of organized energy (soma) separate from other organizations of energy—plants, animals, earth, and oceans. Furthermore, this sensorial way of functioning contributes to the mental image of "I" or "me."

The feeling as well as the belief in a real "me" are virtually inevitable! Regardless of how many philosophers and gurus who, for millennia, have pointed to the illusory reality of the "I," most of us continue to exist in a consciousness totally dedicated to self-centredness.

In some philosophical or religious traditions the goal is to recognize the "I" as an illusion, which brings about the interpretation that we have to get rid of it. However, try as we may, ego is here to stay. The image of oneself is a powerful and necessary representation in our minds. Let us examine further this potentially harmful image.

Hundreds of times a day television commercials, using tantalizing and enticing sales techniques, reinforce the importance of the "me," thus assuring monetary profit for the manufacturers. For example, one commercial concludes with a woman, considered beautiful by our standards, saying, "... [the product] is for the most important person in my life, and that's ME."

Self-concern is a never-ending preoccupation within the content of the thought process. Seeking a "good" self-image is a pernicious, inculcated way of thinking. People suffer because of their unawareness of the consequences of this conditioned thinking. Psychologists understand very well the emotional predicament their clients have to confront; most people going through psychotherapy experience very painful feelings about themselves.

Our egocentric dedication to the aggrandizement, betterment, or comfort of the "me" has given the needed fuel to the forces of industry: manufacturers of cars, drugs, cosmetics, yachts, etc. Of course the real fire is in consumerism, which is also consuming the entire planet. The depletion of natural resources is causing the annihilation of species.

Unfortunately, most people are oblivious to the ominous nature of egocentrism. This is a simple fact, not a derogation of ego.

The reason we are egocentric is that the image of "me," "I," "myself," is very *real* to us.

- We believe we are an entity that we have to protect not only from physical but also from psychological hurts.
- We believe that we must improve ourselves or we will not survive.
- We believe that self-esteem, or its lack, may make us or break us. Do we not have a great number of classes and workshops to improve not only our bodies and our skills, but our *self*-esteem, *self*-reliance, *self*-assertion as well?

It is time that we carefully examine what we mean by "self"—the "me," the "I."

Remember that we need to look:

a) without judgment or evaluation,
b) without the use of learned knowledge (psychology, sociology, etc.) and
c) without attachment to philosophical or religious beliefs.

This does not mean that we have to take an attitude against knowledge. It simply means that we are not using it directly in our inquiry.

We have a general notion or belief that we are body, mind, and spirit. The body with its sensations is our main reality. It exists! We have no question about its actuality.

The existence of mind and spirit seems more nebulous. We cannot definitively say we know the location of the mind, though our experience or our conditioning says that it is in the brain. However, there have been cases of people with very small brain mass who had totally normal mind functions.

The spirit is still more enigmatic and, in general, is real only within belief systems or dogma.

> *Can you answer this question to yourself right now: What and where is the "me," the "I" that is so important to us?*

When answering this question most adults, and definitely children, will point to their bodies. When someone asks, "Who are you?" we usually respond with our name and/or our profession. "I am Joyce." "I am Dr. Taft." But above all, we think of ourselves according to our past. Please notice that I said we *think* of ourselves …

Descartes' famous conclusion comes to mind: I THINK, THEREFORE I AM!

> *What does this statement, presented by this venerable and distinguished philosopher, mean to you?*

Is it possible that it is more correct to say: I AM, THEREFORE I THINK? This poses a very deep and challenging inquiry. While we might not come to any conclusions right now, we can begin to observe how the images of ourselves affect our behavior, our psychophysical health, and our happiness or sense of well-being.

From infancy we learn to refer to our bodies as "I" or "me," as entities different and separate from other bodies: "he," "she," "them." As our image-making function develops, we begin to form images based on our experiences of what we perceive and learn. Through the facility of the memory function we begin to retain, in memory banks, all of our experiences. Our own intelligence begins to gather and organize ideas about "I," "me," "mine," based on these memories. Hence, the *self-image* begins to crystallize.

As infants we did not learn through words; rather we learned through the manner in which we were held and treated. For example, an upset, frustrated mother may call her colicky child "a fussy baby," and handle the infant brusquely. We suppose that the memory of the state of the organism (stomachache), the crying, and the way the infant is treated is associated and retained as memory of *sensations*. Even though no critical words are known in infancy, the sensations of brusque handling may later be associated with judgmental words.

Through conditioning, we learn from very early life to judge this "I," "me," as either *good* or *bad* according to our actions. These classifications depend entirely on the culture in which we are born and by the parents or people raising us. The culture in which they were raised affects us as well—their mores, belief systems, and education. We start to accumulate images of ourselves being "this" or "that" from early childhood. If we had overly-critical people around us we may have built an image of a "me" that is "never right."

We remember the criticisms and begin to incorporate them into our own critical repertoire. We internalize (memorize) the attitudes of those around us and believe them to be true. As we continue to mature, the images become indelibly engraved and therefore ever-present in our memory repositories. By the time we are adults we do not need a parent to criticize us. We have accumulated an arsenal of judgments and evaluations and do an excellent job of it ourselves!

Our own conditioned process is now the critic; and all from memory—FANTASY.

If you are very attentive, you may hear in your mind the *actual voices* of the people who originally criticized you in the past. This takes a special focusing, when you begin to feel relaxed about yourself or when you are in a meditative state of mind—silent, mindful.

> *How does the image of your self arise for you now?*
> *What is your self-image? Have you ever observed?*
> *What do you consider your self to be?*

Let us look at an example of this process. Kurt is a thirty-nine-year-old gentleman in good health, and with a reputation for being a very responsible person. He holds an engineering job at a big company. He is presently divorced and his children are being cared for by his ex-wife. Their relationship could be described as just fair, and there are very tense moments, such as the following one: Kurt has just returned from work and finished talking to his ex-wife on the telephone. "Whenever I talk to her I feel like two cents," he complains aloud to himself, throwing his checkbook on the chair. "I never do anything right for that woman!" Remembering the upset he had with his supervisor today he further laments, "I guess I am wrong about everything these days."

He throws himself on the couch and begins to think about his childhood. "All my life I have had people around me that do not appreciate what or how much I do, or how I do it. There must be something wrong with me!" His reverie brings about some emotions, but he holds back; after all, this is not the first time he has had these feelings. "It's been like this all my life," he thinks to himself. He gets up off the couch, picks up a book on psychology and decides, "I need to better myself. I have to make something of myself." Then he mumbles, "I cannot be just a second-rate engineer all my life. Besides, that woman spends money like water. I am going to need more for the kids when they go to college!"

Because he had made a mistake in his work that day and his supervisor pointed out the seriousness of the error, he feels stupid and despondent. He is sure his supervisor was disappointed in him. On top of that, he has to contend with his wife's complaints about what she considers his inadequacies.

It was the same with his father; he always disappointed his father! "I could never do anything right for him either," he mutters to himself. But he is determined not to let this bother him, so he continues reading his psychology book. This scene of his father's way of treating him as a stupid child is like a repetitious, broken record in Kurt's mind that surfaces and often becomes louder around authority figures. Regardless of all he has achieved in his life, Kurt carries in his mind the self-image of a "stupid guy." He is very concerned with what others think of him. He is a perfectionist and tries very hard to do everything correctly. He is constantly trying to improve himself, to improve his image, while at the same time continually derogating himself in his own mind.

How true is Kurt's image of himself?
How true is the image that others have of Kurt?
How true is the image that Kurt *thinks* others have of him?

> *Have you ever questioned yourself about the*
> *images you carry of yourself? An exploration in*
> *this area may be very useful.*
> *Where is the "I," the "me," that preoccupies*
> *itself with itself?*
> *Is the "me" the organism (the body) that thinks?*
> *Or is the "me" the representation of the*
> *organism's (the body's) mind-function?*
> *Please, inquire.*

If we go back to our earlier exploration of thought and fantasy, we may shed some light on these questions.

We said that all thought is image, representation in the mind. Fantasy, being thought, is also imagery, representation in the mind.

Is the self-image a fantasy?
When we think of ourselves, do we think of ourselves only as a human body?
Or do we think of ourselves as a human body that *behaves* in a certain way?
Or do we think only of our behavior, and therefore the behavior is the "me"?

When we are judging ourselves, do we judge the organism or the behavior?
Which is the "stupid me" or the "smart me," or the "fast-running me"?

Is it the *body*, or the *memory* of what we just did?
Is the "me" the accomplishments—or the mistakes?

Is the self-image an illusion? Is it just a representation in the body/mind?

All of these questions may be easy to answer from any belief system, without giving much attention to the depth of inquiry.

> *But, can you be Socratic in your inquiry, a person who looks deeply for his or her own answer?*
> *Can you answer from your own wisdom?*
> *Have you ever sat quietly, relaxing into contemplation of a question; just being there, simply looking at the question? You might want to try this if you have not done so already.*

If the self-image, the "I" is only a representation in our minds, then when we are despondent about our self-image, are we in fact sad about a fantasy, an illusion? When we are proud of ourselves, are we happy with an image, a representation, a fantasy?

"But the feelings, the emotions are very real!" you may contend. Yes! That is true. We feel the emotions all over our bodies; there are chemical changes that are physiologically traceable.

It does not make sense to have real feelings about an illusion. Does it?

Well, it is the nature of our own functioning to experience the thought process as an actual occurrence, and to believe its content. Thus "I" is very real to us, no matter what anyone says! However, can we trace scientifically where the "I," the "me" resides so that it can be fixed, or changed, or improved?

In regard to improving this "me," what is *that* which we are trying to improve? The mind? The body? The soul? The most common responses to these questions are "my mind" or "my body and my mind." I have heard these answers hundreds of times. What most people are trying to improve is not really their minds but their *own images of themselves in their minds*. I want to contend that we are not *fully aware* of our own humanness, our spiritupsychophysicalness, and so we may be fooling ourselves when we try to improve the "me" *we think we are*, for it is only an image, an illusion.

Perhaps if we could see ourselves just as we came into existence on this earth, we would come to a more clear understanding of the images. In other words, if we could experience ourselves standing naked in the middle of the jungle, divested of acculturation, all titles and roles, we could see that we are simply some of the many beings on the planet; or one of the animal species, if you will, living in relationship with everything that surrounds us. In this scenario there is no need to improve oneself, since no one, as a human being, is better than another; thus, there is no suffering from low self-esteem, or from not being "number one." *No fantasies about ourselves to make us suffer.*

We really do have to wonder if the self-image may be merely an accumulation of memories of our own actions associated with judgments, evaluations, learned titles and roles, such as Father, Elder, Son, Teacher, President, Ph.D., Reverend, Nurse, and so on. It may be that the need for survival is the force that develops any sense of self-image. Roles and titles have been important among people from early times for maintaining order and for survival. Perhaps this is how egocentrism began, and it is now running away with us in the form of fantasy!

Another Way to Look at Self-image

Let us begin with the word "ego" in relationship to fantasy. Webster's New World Dictionary's definition of *ego* is:

1) "The self; the individual as aware of himself;"
2) "egotism, conceit;"
3) "*Philosophy*: the self, variously conceived as a spiritual sub-stance on which experience is superimposed, the series of acts and mental states introspectively recognized, etc."
4) "*Psychoanalysis*: that part of the psyche which experiences the external world through the senses, organizes the thought processes rationally and governs action; it mediates between the instinctual impulses of the id, the demands of the en-vironment and the standards of the superego."

Egocentric means:

1) "Viewing everything in relation to oneself;"
2) "*Philosophy*: existing only as conceived in the individual mind."

As we can see, the meaning of *ego* can be viewed from different avenues of knowledge. The dictionary definitions represent the most common ways we understand self-image, or self-awareness, as ego.

So, ego can be understood in psychoanalysis as *self-awareness*, as a part or function of the mind or psyche, and in philosophy as the *self*, a spiritual substance.

> *How do you view ego? What are your beliefs about it?*

Taking the meanings from the dictionary, we can begin to observe how we are conditioned to see ourselves as ego. We can see the self as a part, a separateness, an entity. We definitely experience ourselves as entities separate from everything else, including our bodies, our emotions, and our thoughts.

In psychoanalytical views, the self or ego is a function of the organism that develops in order to help the individual to cope. It mediates between the organism's needs for survival as well as inner desires (the id) and the demands from the milieu (such as family and society) to conform. The "superego" represents the internalized, inculcated morals and the particular ways, cultural and religious beliefs, and educational standards absorbed from the environment of the individual.

Let us use this explanation for a direct look at ego and the so called superego and id in relationship to fantasy. Remember that these representations in our minds are all very real to us.

As a matter of fact, psychology is a big business; it even has a lobby at the governmental level. Psychological practice is very lucrative these days and so there are many regulations surrounding it. This is important, of course, for the sake of the patient as well as the counselor because without restrictions there would be abuses by charlatans posing as psychologists. Is it not amazing what we can do with our minds? We can create explanations about ourselves, put them into a belief system, corrupt the system, and then make laws to prevent more havoc! This is not a criticism; I am simply calling your attention to the way our minds function.

> *How do you see this? I am not looking for*
> *agreement or disagreement. I am suggesting that*
> *you look at this for yourself.*

Many people have a low regard for ego and are trying very hard to get rid of it in order to be "better." *But is this not more ego?*

Do we have an id, an ego, and a superego?
And if so, where are they?

Are we trying to get rid of a superego? or an id?
How does one get rid of a part of oneself?
What are we improving?
A part of us, called ego?

Despite the hundreds of years of scientific psychological research and practice, we are still very much an unimproved humanity when it comes to the way we live—with competition, wars, and crime. This earth is not becoming a progressively better place in which to live.

We commonly call a person egotistical when he/she is pre-occupied with personal needs and rarely sees the needs of others. The word egotistical represents an exaggerated sense of self-importance. This is again the "me," the "I" we referred to earlier. Therefore, ego is the image of one's self; and as we said before, self-image is a representation in our minds, not actuality. Self-image depends on memory banks. Thus what we call ego is based also on memory, or representation in our minds. Regardless of the elusiveness of these representations, we retain these images through the memory function and play them out as though they were actual. An egocentric or egotistical individual has a kind of mind-set that generates behavior dedicated primarily to self-centered gains.

What are the illusions or fantasies that control the egocentric movements? Let us look at an example:

He was a famous athlete, an actor, and a well-known sports commentator and he had a reputation for being a "good guy." He was a hero to thousands of individuals. But there was a problem: he seemed to have personal marital difficulties. His wife had called the police eight times over a period of several years complaining of his physical abuse. Because of his stature in the community, the police let him go with little more than a reprimand. On one occasion when he was brought to court, he was sentenced to see a psychiatrist and to do community service. Since so many people worshipped him as a hero, the sentence was not enforced.

In other words, he could do whatever he wanted because of his fame. Charges of wife beating were not taken seriously because of his fame and because of *people's belief in the image that had been created in their minds about this hero.*

This person believed his own fantasies of being a good human being who had integrity and high morals. In an interview about morality he expressed this belief very clearly when he said, "I think I am a good person."

Might this mean that "good people" physically assault other human beings? Or might it mean that we have *beliefs about being good human beings*, regardless of our actions?

> *You and I, my friend, have to look thoroughly at our own acculturation, and the content of our consciousness—all our images, including our self-image. In other words, we need to be aware of our own paradigms of thinking, our fantasies, and our personal actions and their consequences, as well as those of humanity at large.*

Summary

1) The self-image is a natural representation in the mind that is reinforced by our sensorial functioning.
2) Ego, or self-image, is part of the function for self-preservation.
3) In Freudian theory the ego is a mediating function between the id (instinct) and the superego (learned morals, etc.).
4) Our own memory function and "conditionability" (ability to condition) contribute to the apparent reality of a self.
5) The commercialization of self-centeredness through the film and television industries has romanticized the importance of self-image to the detriment of the people in society.
6) Believing the hero/heroine fantasy images created by popularity can be detrimental. It can befog the actuality of violence in the behavior displayed by some of these idols.

7.

Painful Memories of the Past

We have been looking at the powerful, "realistic" appearance of self-images. Regardless of how many teachers explain the non-reality of the self-image we carry in our minds, we continue to believe in this "I" we seem to be, with its assigned qualities and defects.

This "I" has a history, retained in the memory banks of each of us. It is important to explore directly, by ourselves, the history of our past and the effects our memories have on our daily conduct and our well-being.

> *What is the past? How do you view it? What do you consider your past or your history?*

If we look closely, we will again see representations in our minds. Each particular memory is in the form of an image or thought in our computer-like memory files. At least this is how we experience their retrieval.

The past is only memory; it does not exist. However, at the moment of recollection we are certain that the emotion, pain, or delight is real, sometimes as real as the original experience itself. The lack of understanding of the *illusive reality* of the memory is what maintains our suffering, rather than the *content* of the memory.

Through psychological theories we have understood or explained our suffering as the direct consequence of our past

43

painful experiences. For example, individuals who have been abused verbally in childhood may carry what they feel to be indelible psychological scars. They may act according to the set of labels they believe themselves to be, such as "stupid," weak," and so on. They may act superior to everyone else and feel inferior inside; or they may act inferior to everyone else, feeling that at least they are not *as bad* as those who would call others stupid. Do you remember the example of Kurt in the previous chapter? His concern with his image was clearly attached to his past experiences.

Suffering and the Past

Many people are depressed because of some traumatic experience they had when they were young. Others become depressed when a loved one dies, and carry the depression for years and years—as long as the memory of the loss lingers. Still others become depressed or ill as a consequence of past abuse. Their behavior and feelings may continue for a lifetime. They are unaware that they are slaves to their memories or to their fantasies of what could have been; thus they miss living the moment of actual life itself.

The morbid, depressed, or painful feelings are experienced as if they were happening again and again. Even though the individuals admit that the triggering event is not happening right now, they feel the anger or the pain of the past as if it were in the moment of now. This is because the mind does not distinguish between stimuli that are self-induced, through memory, and the stimuli received from an outside event. As a result, the feelings are so real that it is difficult for these sufferers to see the truth, which is that *they are living in a world of fantasy.* Even if you point out the truth to them, they dismiss it, saying, "You do not understand;" or, "You don't know what it is to have my pain." In this manner they close the door to inquiry, to the possibilities of a peaceful life, and to a transcendence of their way of functioning.

Marcie was a twenty-nine-year-old woman, divorced with no children. She had been in and out of psychotherapy for the last five years. She was mostly depressed, and while she had never seriously attempted suicide, thoughts about it occupied her mind. "I have never been able to be happy," she complained. "I have been unlucky all my life; my childhood was spent going from foster home to foster home. My adult life has been full of failure. My last relationship with a man left me with a bad taste in my mouth. I can't find any meaning to my life." ... And the memory of the bad experiences haunted her daily.

Every psychotherapist she consulted encouraged her to remember her past, to bring into her experience the affect associated with all the painful events, and to discharge all the emotions. She did this diligently, over and over; still she was again depressed and had gone back to psychotherapy.

When she spoke with me, I asked her if she thought she would commit suicide some day. Her response was in the negative.

"Then why do you think so much about it?" I asked.

"Because I feel like ending this pain," she responded.

"Yes, this is true ... if you put an end to yourself the pain will end too," I said. "They go together, don't they?" (I smiled slightly.)

"Yes," she said, as she laughed. "I don't seem to think I can get rid of the pain without dying."

"Are you fantasizing about how you are going to commit suicide?" I continued.

"Yes, I think about what would happen, what my family would say and do, and my friends, too."

After she described her fantasies I said: "Do you realize how you entertain yourself with these fantasies, how much energy it takes to think and think about them? You don't really want to die. You just want to enjoy your fantasies because they represent the end of your pain. This may be a kind of relief for you. Please look."

Marcie started questioning and observing the content of her fantasies, and after a while she began to see that most of her waking time, as well as her dreams, were filled with thoughts about the painful past or about the future as she would like it to be. She was consumed by her memories and all the emotions that went with them. She had felt them as real—miserable, recurring emotions. But now she began to observe them without judgment or evaluation and could see that she had spent a great deal of time and energy on something that was no longer happening.

"*If it is not happening to you right now it is not reality, it is fantasy,*" I reminded her, and after a while she realized this clearly. This allowed her to experience her past as non-existent, as memory. Thus, the emotions once so real to her began to feel like a dream that no longer needed to be dreamed again. She did not have to continue discharging emotional energy, because the emotions were memories, not occurrences in the present moment. She could begin to enjoy the moment of now and see all the possibilities she had for a new life. This was, for her, the beginning of a new way of functioning.

Marcie and everyone around her could see only a limited way to "cope" with her "problems." In fact there were no real problems, just the fantasy world she was living in, generally considered as *thinking about the past*. Hers is an example of a shift from a somnolent consciousness moving in vicious circles of psychological patterns, to a movement in consciousness that begins to be alive, being more in the moment.

Another case that comes to mind is that of Eli, a young man twenty-five years old, and a student of medicine. He was very intelligent, proud of his scholastic achievements. He was loved and respected by his professors and peers.

He met a young Catholic lady and fell passionately in love with her. They dated a few times. Eli wanted to get married and have children, but she was not sure that was what she wanted. She realized that her heart was in becoming a nun and therefore she severed the relationship. She decided to go to a convent to find out if being a nun was a genuine "calling" for her.

Eli was devastated. He became morose and began to skip his classes. The pain of the loss of his loved one was as intense as the passion he felt for her. He would sit for hours at the beach, fantasizing about what the relationship could have been—the perfect family, the perfect home. He longed for a life as a physician with the perfect wife helping him as a sort of Florence Nightingale. In the past he had expressed these romantic dreams to his beloved, but unfortunately she was no longer there to listen to them. After each cloudless, chimerical fantasy of a future came the memory of her absence, the ghost of rejection, and the emotional pain of his loss. He was sure he would never see her again … and he relived this pain over and over again in his mind. He could hardly do anything but fantasize about the past or the future with his beloved. Eventually he left medical school and I lost communication with him.

This is a typical pattern of romantic love, with its frequent disappointments and tragedies, heard over and over again in popular songs through the ages. Some people's fantasies of possessive love are so real to them that they may culminate in crimes of passion.

Unfortunately, we do not consider remembering the past as "having fantasies." We deal with the past memories as real, giving us real problems.

The director of a halfway house for alcohol and drug abusers in Canada said to me, "The past is something that has really happened to us; we need to understand it and must live with it." … *And live with the past* we do! But for how long, my friends? When are we going to let go of past experiences, which do not exist except in *fantasy*, and *live now*?

We want to deal with what we are discussing here in a compassionate way. When people continue to linger in memories of the past, causing them to be emotionally disturbed or in pathological mental states, we cannot simply say to them, "Oh, you are just fantasizing!" (regardless of how true it may be). That would be disrespectful.

Everyone has to come to the realization of what fantasy is on his or her own, and learn to be able to differentiate between what is a representation in mind from the moment of now (including the appropriate emotions) and what is a representation in mind from memory of the past (including all the emotions associated with it).

We are pointing to the way we function as humans and to the somnolence of our consciousness on the planet. We are so interconnected that it is difficult to get out of the mire of the conditioned consciousness of humanity. In general, we are not aware of our illusions. When we are really willing to *awaken*, to become *totally aware* of our way of functioning, we begin to live *life* rather than the *illusion*.

> *Will you take the challenge of observing yourself
> directly, objectively, which means without
> judgment or evaluations? Are you willing to
> look neutrally at what it means to live the
> illusion of your mind rather than "what is"?
> Are you living the somnolent consciousness of
> humanity, or do you believe you are awakened?
> Are you free from your past, and now living the
> present moment? Or are you still overreacting
> to situations that do not necessarily call for the
> kind or intensity of emotional energy that you
> are experiencing?*

Let this be a gentle, compassionate inquiry of yourself. When we look with neutrality, we are not judging, evaluating, or comparing.

8.

Emotions and Being in the Now

Emotions are psychophysiological movements of energy in the human organism.

We usually define emotion as an intense feeling or response or reaction (to a person or a situation or a memory).

Webster's New World Dictionary defines *emotion* as:

1) "Strong feeling; excitement; the state or capability of having the feelings aroused to the point of awareness;"
2) "complex reactions with both physical and mental manifestations such as love, hate, fear, anger, etc."

The second meaning points to the fact that the thought process is bonded with the physical components of emotions; these emotional responses are measurable through the skin, muscles, blood pressure, and brain activity. Furthermore, we can become psychophysically upset, or thrilled, at a *mere thought*, a fantasy. We will become depressed upon imagining a dangerous situation (impending doom) or the memory of the death of a dear one; or we will be elated while imagining a fortuitous event.

Many people would say that emotions may be felt (conscious) or suppressed or repressed (unconscious). I, however, would like to contend that emotions are experienced consciously, and that what we call suppressed or repressed emotions are only memories of the emotional activity of the past. In other words, the movement of energy we call emotion is felt consciously, giving the impression of a *reality* to the emotion in the present moment. It feels as if it is happening *now*. The pain of the rejection of a loved one may be just as intense when being remembered as it was at the first moment of cognizance of the great loss. That was clear in the case of Eli. He continued reliving the phantasm of his lady friend's rejection, suffering to the point of not being able to continue his medical studies.

Given the way we function in representations—thought, memory, fantasy—it follows that the process of psychotherapy would be dedicated to remembrance and abreaction (the process of relieving repressed emotions). Most of us believe that by bringing into consciousness suppressed or repressed material we can discharge the emotional energy and feel better.

And … we feel better when we express our emotions, don't we? …
Unless we are discharging anger and someone gets hurt …
Then we feel bad again (guilty) …
Then, of course we apologize, or ask for forgiveness, and feel better again …
Until the next time when we "get mad," and we feel bad again … and so on ad infinitum.
What a merry-go-round!

Still, we believe in expressing emotions for the sake of our well-being. Doctors recommend that we not withhold our feelings, because being in a constant state of inner tension, of emotional upheaval, may cause damage to the organism. Indeed, we know that continual tension causes high blood pressure, heart disease, excessive production of gastric juices (ulcers), migraines, and so on.

Through the psychotherapeutic method many people become more expressive, thus alleviating their tensions. In traditional psychoanalysis, the individual goes back as far as he or she can into childhood and brings to consciousness all memories from the past that are retrievable, as well as the affect (emotions associated with events). At this point the person relives the unconscious content by remembering all the details and emotions as if they were happening in the present. The analyst then makes constructs or explanations according to his/her theoretical orientation (Freud, Jung, etc.). It is an arduous process that can take five to ten years, depending on the individual and the frequency of the sessions.

If the psychoanalysis is complete and successful, individuals may feel relieved and may understand their problems better; at least they can explain to themselves and others why they feel or act the way they do. This does not mean that they will never be bothered with emotions of rage or sadness or despair or fear; it simply means that they can cope better and in a more adult manner than they did before the psychotherapeutic process. Thus they are considered by the doctor and themselves as being well, or no longer neurotic.

Through the expertise of the analyst, this objective is achieved by the *natural thinking-fantasizing* process being directed in a certain way. By bringing the client to a different way of viewing the past and by creating new attitudes and ways to cope, one could say that new ways of thinking are established, and perhaps new neuron pathways develop in the brain.

The point of interest for us here is that the same function that produces the suffering also produces the cure or betterment—namely, the thought/fantasy process, the representations in the mind. It is for this reason that psychotherapy works for a majority of people who seriously wish to do something about their emotional quagmire.

> *Have you thought about the fact that if you are depressed and you wish to change your predicament, the answer is within you—in that same system that keeps you in a vicious cycle of emotional morass?*

To experience the *living truth* of this may be very freeing. By living truth I mean not just the intellectual knowledge of it as a fact, but the experience at the gut level, in your heart of hearts, that *you and only you* are responsible for the representations in your mind. Furthermore, you feel deeply the responsibility of living life *now*, not the illusion of your past memories or fantasies.

I have described one of the many psychotherapeutic methods being used (the longest, most complex, and thorough method I know and also one of the oldest). However, there are many short and effective kinds of psychotherapeutic approaches that seem to be successful for many people.

A few years ago I met a physician who was using guided imagery with his patients to, as he said, "transform the past" of the sufferers. By means of imagery, fantasy, the patients would choose the way they wanted their past to *have been*. In this manner, he claimed, they created a new set of memories to recall. He never said that the old memories were erased. I met some of his enthusiastic patients, who claimed that the method had "worked" for them. Given the power of fantasy, it might have helped them to cope, at least temporarily.

While guided imagery and psychotherapy work to *alleviate* the emotional state or condition, and people live more comfortable lives, these procedures do not seem to really *transform* human beings or the consciousness of humanity at large. We remain in the same movement of consciousness that caused the suffering in the first place. This does not diminish the value of either guided imagery or psychotherapy. Apparently, according to the testimony of people undergoing psychotherapeutic processes, these methods help to alleviate the emotional upheavals brought about by the *past*.

You might be wondering if all psychotherapists work only with the *past*. Are there not some psychotherapeutic methods that deal with current problems in living? And dealing with current problems is dealing with the *present*, is it not?

If you are asking these questions, you are right in thinking that the most recent psychological approaches deal with current issues. Even amateur psychotherapist television hosts and hostesses are climbing on that bandwagon! However, *anything we talk about will be in the past, even if it is as recent as a minute ago.*

Have you noticed that we are always speaking
about past or future because the moment of now
is so elusive? By the time you say something is
happening now, it has already happened. It's
already in the past!

It is of great importance to become fully aware that what we call the present moment is just as elusive as the past or the future. This awareness clarifies our understanding of the nature of thought, fantasy, and remembered emotions.

When we recall events and emotions, we are thinking; we have images, or as we said earlier, we have representations in the mind.

When we are thinking of what we are doing in the present, we are also remembering. To illustrate, try the following experiment: Bring your hands together and make a sound. Think of the sound the very instant you hear it. By the time you think about it, it is no longer the same instant. This brings up some questions: Are we ever in the present? Is thought only memory? What is time? How did we arrive at the concept of time? Is time an illusion? Of course, to give my own answers or conclusions to these questions would be to curtail the readers' ability to inquire and discover for themselves. It would defeat the purpose of this book.

If you have never before asked these questions,
you might find it very enlightening to
contemplate the nature of time in relationship to
thought and emotions. Without using acquired
knowledge, inquire directly, using your wisdom.

The thought process is cognizance, a function manifested in consciousness that seems to be too slow to catch up with the nanosecond—*the moment of life itself.* By the time we think about something, a billionth of a second has elapsed, and we are already in the past. We seem to be doomed to live in the past. Our saving grace is the fact that we can also intuitively experience *full awareness* or *insights*, which are manifested in consciousness as well, but are beyond the thought process.

Insight, or *full awareness*, belongs to the realm of intuition. Dr. Deepak Chopra says: "Intuition is not thought, it is the non-local cosmic field of information that is whispered to you in silence, between your thoughts."[1] I very much agree that intuition is not thought. *True, total, or full awareness is the cosmic field of information coming into our consciousness, and it comes out of the silence that is Space. I call this our saving grace, because it is actual Bliss!*

However, I disagree with Dr. Chopra's statement that intuition occurs in the silence between thoughts. Rather than being "in between" thoughts, insight or full awareness is more like an impact that obstructs, temporarily, the ongoing linear movement of thought. My sense is that thought is a localized event, while insight or awareness is a non-local event, therefore outside of the time/space realm of our thinking process.

Even though thought is the medium by which we relate or communicate insights or awareness, the insights in themselves are not bound by time. They are very fleeting moments of experience that are usually difficult to put into words. *Full awareness* may manifest as an image, a vision that may or may not be accompanied by sensations or feelings. Any sensations or feelings are after the fact. Awareness occurs with the speed of lightning and is not illusory. It has a transforming effect in the whole organism, for it is a microcosmic event having an effect at the cellular level.

Full awareness, insight, is a complete experience that generally leaves a representation in mind (thought). An intellectual or emotional experience is incomplete and limited in consciousness. It is mainly a representation in mind that affects but *does not transform* the organism. In other words, full awareness or insight is transcendental, while thinking and feeling are not.

We sometimes have "realizations" that appear to be intuition, awareness. However, they are rather a kind of rearrangement of

[1] "The Higher Self", audiotape series by Deepak Chopra (Nightingale Conant Corporation, Niles, Illinois).

the information we already have; these rearrangements allow us to better understand something, but we are hardly ever truly transformed by them. Nevertheless they make a change in the organism, as thought does, and people feel improved. It is my contention that not all so-called intuitions are transcendental in nature. Full, total awareness or insight (intuition) is transcendental and the true whisper of the cosmos, space, or God, if you will. It emanates from the silence that is the Unmanifest, or God.

It is possible to experience a *state of being* where there is no suffering from past emotional upheavals. In order to live a life where the present experiences and their corresponding emotions are not left to be dealt with in a distant future, one has to be *aware, awake* to the total experience of each emotion *as it is happening*.

This means that one has to:

- feel completely every *sensation*;
- feel completely every *feeling*;
- be totally alert to every furtive *memory* that is present in the content of the mind;
- be totally alert to the elaboration of the thought process;
- be totally alert to the *fantasies*; and
- be totally aware of the *other*, and of the universe as well.

To experience ourselves in this manner is transformational. Our relationships also transform, because emotions are experienced quickly and totally. We begin to communicate immediately and appropriately as needed, according to the event of the moment. That is, the perception of the present situation is not clouded by the network of past memories—past conditioning. Any misunderstanding is clarified through true communication; there are no resentments or emotional memories to put into files. There is no need to rehearse (fantasize) what we are going to say to someone when we meet or confront them, because the communication is spontaneous and complete at the time of the incident.

In a situation where we cannot communicate immediately

with the person with whom we are in conflict, the emotions are still experienced in their totality in the present moment; the memory of the situation is put in abeyance only until the appropriate time for communication presents itself. There are no vestiges, because fantasies are not elaborated. There are no rehearsals of what to say, because we are not emotionally charged, as it were. We do not feel frustrated since there is nothing to discharge; all the emotions have been experienced totally. *When we live in the present, we are very clear that we do not know what the circumstances will be in the future, nor what we are really going to say.*

It is very freeing to know directly, to be insightful of how we function in emotions, memories, fantasy, and imagination—representations. It is liberating to be fully aware of the potential for transformation in our way of living. To experience ourselves in this kind of totality, in the moment of life itself, is insightful living—a transformation in consciousness.

I am describing what it is to live in total responsibility. When we experience a transcendent consciousness, our way of living becomes very harmonious, for we are enjoying peace of mind.

In a transformed, awakened, aware consciousness, the ground of being is equanimity. Life is lived in the moment of *now*, rather than in the illusion created by our own natural process. This state of being can be discovered through insight. *Insight, intuition, and transcendence* are natural human processes, available in the energy of the universe, which we are.

> *I would like to remind you that these statements*
> *are not to be believed or disbelieved, but to be*
> *used as stimuli for your own inquiry.*

9.

The Quest for the Perfect Relationship

There is a very destructive fantasy which haunts young and old alike: the quest for the perfect relationship, based on the image of the perfect lover, the perfect husband, the perfect wife, the perfect partner. It is the relationship portrayed in the romantic novel, the romantic movie, and television soap operas.

Even though movies and novels are more and more dedicated to the depiction of so-called reality in relationships, the public always prefers the romantic ending. Even a tragic ending is romanticized, because it agrees with the conditioned romantic fantasies of the general public. Movie producers fear the loss of millions of dollars if their productions fail to satisfy the general public. The monetary gain is more important to them than any contribution to society's well-being.

While there are some small companies dedicated to raising the awareness for the need of new paradigms in thinking, such as the company that produced *Mindwalk* (Capra), they are the small minority. Most are large corporations maintaining the fantasy world by "popular demand." The mental conditioning in our culture manipulates the industries and maintains the vicious circles of our somnolent consciousness. Our habitual demands prevent fullness of human awareness.

The Eternal Quest

Marie is a fifty-six-year-old secretary, presently divorced. She says, "I have been married twice to similar people, but this time I will pick the right one. I have learned a lot from these relationships. For one thing, I see that I fooled myself, thinking that each relationship was the one I was looking for. They seemed to be just what I wanted ... until we married, and then, oh boy!"

Both of her marriages had been to men she described as domineering. She disliked that trait, but as she says, "They were demonstrative and loving when they were not angry." She confides, "During our courtship each of them was romantic and gentleman-like, you know, always opening the car door, bringing me roses ... we had such good times." At this point she begins to fight her tears, saying, "I miss that in my life! I miss a warm hug when I come home."

But then she begins remembering the bad times. "I don't miss my first husband's bad temper, or my last husband's drinking and getting violent, but I miss the nice things they did when they were in a good mood!" And the tears start.

Now Marie is on the quest for a new relationship that will satisfy her need to be courted; that is the part she likes the best. When I asked her to make a list of all she wanted in her future relationship she described it thus:

"He must be good looking, because I could not go to bed with an ugly guy. He must be able to be in charge of things and take care of me, but let me do what I want. He must have enough money for us to travel. He must be very warm and cuddly, kind of romantic and, hopefully, a good dancer. He must be fun—a fun person. Not serious like an older man. I do not mean he has to be a young man either; just about my age, more or less.

"I don't want someone who is argumentative, I do not care about having discussions about politics and religions, that sort of thing. But he must be a good conversationalist; otherwise it could be boring! I don't want somebody who is not in touch with their emotions. I cannot tolerate that!"

With both husbands, she admits today, she had been the submissive, admiring girl during the courting period. She did not complain about certain things such as their lack of feelings or, in the case of her second husband, his excessive drinking. But once they were married, she said, "I let them have it! Some things I wasn't about to tolerate! Of course then the fights started!"

Her complaints about her husbands were numerous and repetitious. But she believed she had learned her lessons, and could now find the kind of man she really wanted … And so she found a "wonderful man" who was "different and sensitive."

However, a year or so later she was back into her drama. "He is so needy that nothing is left for me," she said in tears. She was disappointed and totally devastated. She looked tired and old for her years, and she felt ill. "I know I have to leave the relationship, but I am so lonely without one! I have to find a better relationship; I know it is out there!"

The last time I spoke with her she was more aware of her patterns but unwilling to let go of her emotional attachment to them.

If we look at Marie's list of the description of her dream man we see that she is still thinking like an adolescent. She wants all the qualities of Prince Charming. She still wants to dance and have a good time. She actually wants a person who will woo her, take care of her and let her do what she wants. Her demeanor is that of a teenager. Marie's way of thinking and the description of her desired future husband lack a mature view of marriage and the mutual responsibility of two adults in relationship.

The Maries of this world can never find the man they think they want, because what they look for is really a duplication of their own fantasy. The men of fantasies are non-existent. They are the Prince Charmings of an illusory world that is reinforced by traditions, novels, and movies.

Juan was fifty years old, a very elegant looking and healthy man. He was a widower who had dated several women in the last year. "What is happening to women?" he would complain to his best friend Joe. "They are so forward and demanding, it is disgusting! They invite you to dinner and serve you frozen food because they don't want to cook. Then they expect you to help with the dishes. That's a woman's job. What happened to femininity?"

Juan wanted to marry a woman who would take care of him and satisfy all his needs. "My wife and I had a perfect relationship. She was warm and intelligent and not demanding at all," he used to tell Joe. "I would love to find a person like her. It seems as though most ladies today want to tell you what to do all the time. I was the king of my castle! Elena made me feel like I was royalty. She sure was a good woman!"

This is how Juan remembered Elena, his wife. He had an image of her being all he wanted her to be for him. He had somehow forgotten or denied all the arguments and disappointments he had experienced during their long marriage. Now he was looking for the perfect Elena of his dreams, and was frustrated to find women so different from his fantasy. All he could do was complain.

People like Marie and Juan remain stuck in their thinking, believing that some day their fantasies may come true. In the meantime they miss life and the beauty of nurturing, mature relationships because they cannot appreciate people just as they are. When they meet someone, all they can do is compare the person to the image of their desires. Of course, these images rarely match the person before them, and they are disappointed.

Our psychotherapeutic techniques attempt to bring people to face "reality" in their relationships and to compromise. They do not focus on eliminating the perpetuation of fantasy in the culture. We think that to satisfy our own needs is a must, and to satisfy each other's emotional needs is what is expected in relationships. To have a dream is accepted, especially in our culture, and to pursue the dream is considered virtuous. We are not aware that we are tacitly encouraging fantasy.

Fantasy paralyzes the process of maturing of individuals. We elaborate images and create fantasies that keep us in personal, vicious circles of conditioned psychological patterns. Thus these patterns are perpetuated in humanity's consciousness.

Emotional Maturity and Relationships

When emotions are reactions from past memories, our relationships are not harmonious or nurturing. However, when the people involved in a relationship are in a process of synchronized change (becoming mature) they can see each other *as they are*, not according to the emotional images of the past, or fantasies.

Unfortunately not all people in relationship develop synchronistically; therefore one person may change, become more mature, and the other remain immature. This often happens to couples and to parents and children.

For example, a father or a mother may be so concerned with work, climbing the ladder of success in their company, that they are often away when they are needed at home to care for their young children. Often the care is relegated to strangers who do not have the ability or the compassion to see the children through difficulties. This is an eternal conflict in our modern society. Many youngsters are left with great resentments, sometimes carried for a lifetime in their memory banks.

Sometimes these parents unfold rapidly through a shift in consciousness, and their attitudes and philosophical or religious views change drastically. They recognize that they were very negligent of their children in early years and they usually acknowledge their mistake as they become more loving and understanding. The children may accept the apology superficially, but continue to see the parents through the past resentments.

Sometimes these parents prefer to live away, by themselves or with new companions or friends who share their new philosophical approach to life. The children may continue to be somewhat bitter and in their minds (their fantasies) they continue to feel neglected. "If they really cared for us," they reason, "they would live with us, or at least close by instead of living with their friends." They do not allow the new warmth from their parents to touch them, regardless of the present loving behavior of their parents. These offspring remain immature, unhappy and resentful, interpreting (through their fantasies) the parent's new life style as a repetition of the early patterns they considered *neglect*.

Similarly, young people may have a shift in consciousness while the parents remain in the mire of their fantasies, their conditioned consciousness. They, too, prefer to live away on their own. The now-adult offspring may have an attitude of wholeness about raising their own children, about ecology, and about their spiritual faith. In other words, their paradigm of thinking is no longer the conditioned paradigm of their parents.

The parents cannot accept the children's new way of life and continuously find something to criticize, just as they did when the children were "rebellious" youth (these are the parents' thoughts). The interpretation is elaborated through their memory repertoire and fantasies, which continue to haunt them.

When members of a family do not mature synchronously, the memories of the past, fantasies, act as barriers to harmony and love.

It is our nature to function with images and memory. From infancy we begin to build images and accumulate experiences in our computer-like, memory windows. Therefore, most people live their personal relationships accumulating images and memories, preserving them to use as their ground of being throughout life. The past is the network for their conditioned way of behaving. The memories from the past color their opinions, likes, dislikes, attitudes, beliefs—everything they listen to and do. They actually inherit this conditioning from their progenitors and in turn pass it to the next generation in a chain, perpetuating paradigms of thinking in the consciousness of humanity.

Fantasies May Veil Emotional Needs

Sometimes fantasy may help veil emotional needs and conflicts between people. Let me relate a case I witnessed.

Peggy and Ed married young, and after five years of marriage they had a beautiful baby boy. Ed's company transferred him to two different states during these five years of marriage, and they had to buy and sell their house each time they were relocated by the company. Every time they looked for a house they had disagreements. Peggy wanted a larger house than Ed. However, needing to stay within a budget, they settled for a smaller house.

Ed was relocated a third time and again they had to find a new home. Since the baby was getting bigger and they had plans for a larger family, Ed conceded that this time they needed a bigger house. Peggy was delighted, and she diligently and enthusiastically looked for a house in this new city. She fell in love with a house on the outskirts of the metropolitan area. "It is my dream house!" she told Ed. "We have space for everything there, including all the paraphernalia for your hobbies. It is surrounded by trees, and it has a big yard for the kids!" The house was four thousand square feet, with everything she had always wanted, including four bathrooms. She could picture herself and the big family they were going to have in this beautiful house. Peggy loved to decorate and she embarked on fantasies of creating a "House Beautiful." It was wonderful!

Ed was reluctant. It was a little more expensive than his financial calculations allowed for a house. However, Peggy was so enthusiastic, the house was beautiful, and they could afford it if he just cut down on something else in his budget, like his gun and bicycle collections.

Peggy's enthusiastic fantasies and Ed's fantasy of being the rich man seduced the couple into getting the house of their dreams. They both worked feverishly to get the house in order and prepare for a housewarming to entertain their friends and proudly display their dream house. They were delighted with their own accomplishments and possessions.

Six months after they had moved, Peggy was beginning to complain to Ed that she needed help from him to keep the house clean and neat; she was busy with the baby most of the time and the house was too big for her to clean by herself. To add to the conflict, Ed was spending more time traveling and less time at home than before.

The beautiful house dream was tumbling down quickly for Peggy as she faced the actualities and responsibilities of having a large house. The couple began having more difficulties as time went by. Even though they hired a housekeeper to help once a week, Peggy still felt that there was too much for her to do alone. Ed, on the other hand, felt she should have thought of this before they bought the house. "I told you it was too big, but you wouldn't hear of it!" he would complain. "I have to work to keep up with the expenses of this house. I can't just stay home when you want me to." Her usual response was, "It is not that you are gone so much, but the fact that when you are home you do not help me. That is what infuriates me! You love to show off your beautiful house to your friends and working buddies, but I have to keep up with everything so that it is decent when they come traipsing in to play pool with you!" This kind of conflict became more common in their daily routine.

Peggy's fantasy of a big house was actually concealing a desire for a closer relationship with her husband. In her own mind, a big house would make them work more closely together, just as they did when they first moved in. "We were so happy getting the house together!" she confessed. "That is what I really wanted. A place where we could work together, building a *real home*. Instead, he is traveling more often, leaving me alone, and when he is home he cares more about his buddies than the house and his family!"

Fantasies often serve more than one purpose. In this case Peggy was absorbed with the "House Beautiful" magazine dream, while emotionally she hoped that getting a big house would bring a change in the relationship with her husband. After all, her parents had moved to a large house when she was ten years old, and she remembered very clearly how her mother and father worked together to keep up their place. She had wonderful memories of living in a large home and being very happy. The memories from the past contributed to the creation of fantasies about a big house being a panacea for her present circumstance. Unfortunately, her present house was not like the house of her memories. It was beginning to be a source of suffering.

Summary

- When our relationships are based on fantasy we can expect disappointment and suffering.
- When our relationships are based on needs rather than unconditional love, we can only hope for compromise and tolerance.
- When our relationships are based on our conditioned preferences, we are bound by the invisible ties of our prejudice, the inculcated fantasy of the Prince Charming tales, and the ever-illusory romance of novels and movies.
- Healthy relationships evolve when our love for others is unconditional.
- In healthy relationships we see the other as he/she is, without judgment or evaluation, and without demand for change. Furthermore, we see ourselves in an equally responsible manner.

10.

Fear, Anxiety, Panic, and Fantasy

Fear

Fear is a natural human reaction, defined in Webster's Third New International Unabridged Dictionary as "an unpleasant emotional state characterized by anticipation of pain or great distress and accompanied by heightened autonomic activity, especially involving the nervous system." This definition reflects the general unfavorable attitude we carry about fear. Thousands of books have been written on this "unpleasant" emotion, most of them attempts to either cope with, resolve, alleviate, or terminate fear. In this book, we want to approach the subject from a commonsense view and according to a neutral observation of our ways of functioning and our conditioning.

Webster's New World Dictionary of the American Language defines *fear* as:

1) "a feeling of anxiety and agitation caused by the presence or nearness of danger, pain, evil etc.;"
2) "to feel reverence or awe for (someone);"
3) "to expect with misgiving."

Regardless of how much we understand or accept our emotions or how much psychotherapy we have experienced, fear (or anxiety or agitation, as offered by the dictionary) seems to remain unwanted. We continually attempt to unburden ourselves of this emotion. It is my contention that we cannot get rid of what we call fear per se, because it is a natural psychophysical, purposive reaction. The "fight or flight" response, observable in animals and humans, derives from the natural survival and protective mechanisms that perpetuate the species. At the perception of any stimuli interpreted as threatening, the whole organism responds with all the needed chemistry and muscle tension for the body to spring into action as needed. This is a healthy and natural way of functioning on this planet.

The apprehensiveness and attention that occurs when we are faced with danger is a natural protective activity for which we may be grateful. It helps us to survive! We call this being afraid, and because of the discomfort we feel—actually this is our interpretation—we try to get rid of it, rather than to inquire and perhaps gain some insight into the nature of what we call fear.

People often tell me that they would like to "get rid of" or "have no more" fears. They want to end fear before it occurs again. They are not aware of their *fear of being afraid*. In other words, their fantasy is to get rid of something they call fear, which *may* happen in the future. Since this is fantasy, it might easily be dissolved if they understood deeply the interrelatedness of fear and fantasy.

Not everyone reacts in the same way when fear strikes. We behave according to the way we have been conditioned from early childhood and according to our predispositions. That is, we may have inherited a tendency toward very fast or very slow reactions, or panicky behavior. Observing infants is an education in how we are predisposed to a particular way of reacting as well as in how we humans become conditioned. For example, my grandchild has already adopted mannerisms that are typical of his parents. If I hurt my hand and say something like, "Ouch!" he immediately responds, "Are you okay? Let me kiss it!" My friend's child at six months would turn his face away and sometimes cry when a stranger approached him. His brother, on the other hand, was always smiling no matter who came near him. These behaviors may later become mind-sets in some children.

When we are afraid, we experience a multiplicity of sensations, feelings, and thoughts which, in themselves, are not painful or uncomfortable. They are neutral. Upon the sight of danger we are going to experience a naturally faster heartbeat, general tension in the muscles, elevation of blood pressure, a surge of adrenaline, and other less perceptible, subtle changes in the organism. These changes in themselves are not unpleasant. They may be the same alterations we feel in a moment of exhilaration when we meet a lover, when we receive good news, or when we win a tournament.

What is it that makes us experience this combination of sensations as unpleasant at one time and not at another? Is the difference:

- the content of the mind?
- the type of thought?
- the quality of thought?
- the endless associations to past memories?
- the way we were conditioned to *interpret* these physical reactions?

> *How do you see this? Have you thought about it*
> *before? Can you see any difference in the*
> *processes per se of your own feelings, sensations,*
> *and thoughts in the moments of exhilaration,*
> *from those in the moments of fear? (The focus is*
> *on the processes only.)*

Whether there is an *actual* danger or an *imagined* one, our whole organism becomes ready to take action to protect itself. Dr. Jeanne Achtenberg, referring to the physiology of fear, explains in her book *Imagery and Healing*, "The danger, of course, need not be 'out there,' but only fantasized. Vivid mental images of a nuclear attack are completely capable of eliciting a fear response." The fears most people feel are not based on an actual danger or threat to their well-being. Most of the time people are afraid due to their *images*, their *fantasies* of what *could* happen.

We could learn some lessons from primitive people living in the jungles or from animals in the savannas. Animals become totally alert when a predator comes into view or range of scent. However, they do not start running unless the predator is on a hunt. On the contrary, they stay quietly alert; for example, while a predator such as a lion or a cheetah proceeds to the water hole for a drink, other animals such as zebras and gazelles simply look on. They do not panic at the mere sight of a predator.

Similarly, when hunting or fishing in rivers of the jungle, primitive people are constantly alert to sudden noises or the rustling of leaves. Their demeanor is no more than an alertness, with a readiness for action. They do not seem to have an aversion to what they are experiencing. They do not immediately start running; they do not seem to elaborate a fantasy about what *could* happen. If they hear the sound of an animal but there is no threat of attack, they might simply make a comment, as they accept the probability that a creature (snake, monkey, etc.) is going by. I call this a natural reaction, or healthy *fear* (if we insist on using this word).

Contrary to this, most people in our civilization have been conditioned to fear, and have developed unnecessary anxieties. The *natural* alertness and readiness for action has changed. Due to the many dangers we have created through our technological progress, we have had to build an *unnatural* sense of protection against *unnatural* technical monsters. For example, we often instill fear in children when teaching them to cross a street. We do not mean to scare them, but we are so afraid of what may happen to them that they pick up our fearful state of mind as if by osmosis; of course, they also become afraid of what *could* happen to them. And the inculcating cycle of conditioning to fear goes on.

The increasing crime rate in the cities of the United States is truly alarming; many young people are so frightened of attacks from other youngsters that they carry guns to school. They are in a constant state of excitement and anxiety. Furthermore, the development of nuclear weapons and the hydrogen bomb has caused all kinds of fear throughout the world. I have heard many young people say that they are afraid they are "to be witness to a nuclear holocaust."

We can no longer say that we live *the natural life* of this planet, which is to be in harmony with nature!

> *Would you look at what you call fear? What do*
> *you experience when you think you are afraid:*
> *emotions, sensations, images?*

It is important to become fully aware of the relationship of fear to fantasy so that we may enjoy our truly natural way of being as members of the human species. For this purpose, we need to differentiate between the natural, spontaneous, alert re-actions we experience when faced with a valid threat (normally called fear) and the more destructive states we usually refer to as anxiety, panic, and phobias (exaggerated fears).

Panic Attacks

Panic attacks are sudden occurrences that feel so real and fierce that the person may become irrational. Let us look into a panic scene. Rosie is driving to the new shopping mall where there are many trees and open spaces. It is a beautiful day for shopping in this wonderful place full of things Rosie wants. She thinks about how she will enjoy being able to see the blue sky today while she shops for the pretty shoes she saw advertised in the newspaper. Her reverie is full of wonderful scenes about the dinner-dance Saturday night and the high-heel shoes that will enhance the beauty of her legs while she dances. However, her fantasy scenario is abruptly interrupted and she sees herself lying on the dance floor with other people that are dead. She cringes for a split second, but the chilling flash disappears and she automatically turns the radio on loudly, and begins happily singing to the music. She arrives at the mall and begins to look at the shoes displayed inside the windows. Suddenly she is grasped by a horrendous fear. Her body is trembling, she has burst into a cold sweat, and her heart is pounding so hard she thinks it is coming out of her chest. Quickly returning to the car, she heads for home. Her whole body is in a state of panic; the sensations are mercilessly overpowering and she feels as though she is going to die. At the same time her mind is full of fantasies: "What is wrong with me? I must have cancer, maybe a tumor in my brain, maybe I am going crazy." The endless imagery intensifies the original sensation of panic. Having no awareness that a tragic memory from the past mixed with her fantasies of the dinner-dance had triggered the panic, and feeling out of control, Rosie turns the car around and goes to the nearest hospital where she is treated with medications. Since Rosie has no recollection of the dreadful memory flare-up, she does not indicate to the doctor that there might be a psychological reason for her attack. Not finding anything seriously wrong physically, the doctor recommends further testing.

Rosie is one of those people who, at this point, has tried different kinds of remedies and psychotherapy for only short periods of time. Her outlook is not spiritual in nature, and she has refused her best friend's suggestions of biofeedback, relaxation, and meditation. These therapeutic modalities are often beneficial for anxiety and panic attacks, because with their help the sufferers get in touch with their own capability to relax the body/mind at any time. When they are used in conjunction with inquiry into one's own true nature, they can open doors to spiritual, peaceful, healthy living. There are thousands of Rosies in the world who are closed or opposed to any suggestions. They can only continue to cope and remain ignorant of any other alternatives, except the ones determined by their conditioned way of thinking.

Phobias

Phobias are irrational, persistent fears based on past memories. Like panic attacks, they are associated with fantasies. If the phobia is about heights, the person is sure he or she will fall if they go to the mountains or the top of a tall building or any place where they are high above the ground. Some people are afraid to travel, so they remain at home most of the time, going out only when it is absolutely necessary. After a few years of experiencing phobias, the fear becomes so overpoweringly real that some individuals, in order to protect themselves from their imaginary doom, will not leave their houses at all.

Pauline was a sixty-year-old woman in good health. She had never married and she lived with an aunt in a small house. She had stayed inside her house for thirty years. She was so phobic about going beyond the limits of the walls of her house that she only knew the world around her by looking through the windows. She was afraid something would happen to her if she went outdoors. Her original phobia involved cars. She had been hit by a car at the age of twenty-nine, and she feared her life was in danger in the streets. She never forgot that trauma, and had made a decision to never leave her house again and take chances. Her original phobia had generalized into other fears, such as that of someone attacking her if she were to go outdoors. She felt very safe inside her made-up prison. She had all kinds of fantasies about "what could happen" and she believed them to be most probable.

When she was approached by a member of her family to seek therapy for the phobia, she refused help. Her aunt provided for her and took care of the outside chores; Pauline took care of the work inside. They said that they had "managed well for thirty years" and they were "satisfied to live in this manner."

Pauline had adjusted to living a more comfortable life by not challenging her mental set. She did not have to suffer from her imaginings as long as she kept a familiar daily routine. But if she did anything that brought up associations to any of her fantasies of doom, she would feel terrified, "as if she was hanging by her little pinkie over a cliff," her aunt would explain. Pauline was relatively well as long as she stayed within her self-imposed *imaginary* boundaries. She was always assured, by her fantasies of *safety*, that she would be all right as long as she was inside her house. She vehemently believed this fantasy, without considering other possibilities. Pauline was trapped between fantasies of doom and fantasies of safety.

Other common phobias involve insects or animals. Whenever they are in a situation with the object of their phobia, sufferers of these phobias become petrified and are unable to function. Their feeling of impending doom is so real at that moment that they cannot distinguish between their *imagination* and *what is*.

One of the best treatments for phobic people is to reintroduce the object of their phobia, slowly bringing the *truth of what is* to their awareness. This process is called de-sensitization and it involves introducing the object of the phobia to the person ever so slowly, so that the sufferer can reacquaint her/himself with it. At the same time the person has the opportunity to experience his or her extreme fear in a very controlled and safe environment, which allows the realization of the exaggeration of feelings and sensations in relationship to the actuality of the event. In this manner the phobic person begins to distinguish fantasy from fact.

It is important to observe that *within the mind process, there is a belief in its own content*. In other words, *we believe our own imagination*.

Persons suffering from phobias are prisoners of their own images, prisoners of their own minds. Fantasy is their killer. They are more dead than alive. They can never experience the joy of life itself because they believe their own fantasies.

Anxiety

To the health professional, anxiety has a particular meaning: a fearful feeling that is unfounded in reality. To people in general it may have different personal meanings. Most people, however, have one thing in common: a dislike for anxiety.

Since this is a *commonsense* book, I will use, as before, the conventional dictionary meanings rather than definitions from

any particular psychological or medical approaches. From Webster's New World Dictionary:
Anxiety:

1) "A state of being uneasy, apprehensive or worried about what may happen; concern about a possible future event;"
2) "*Psychiatry*: an intense state of this kind, characterized by varying degrees of emotional disturbance and psychic tension;"
3) "an eager but often uneasy desire (anxiety to do well)."

The first meaning alludes to the association to imagination or fantasy: "… being uneasy, apprehensive or worried about what may happen." The apprehensive state is due to the elaboration of thought (fantasy), the imagining of some dreadful event in the future. People suffer from anxiety because they *believe* their images, their fantasies. Let us turn to an example:

Alexander is a forty-three-year-old married man working at an allopathic medical clinic as a psychotherapist. He is a graduate of Yale and enjoys a good reputation among his family and peers as a responsible person. He is affable, well liked by the patients, and appears to be well adjusted and balanced. However, Alexander, like some of the patients in his clinic, takes Valium for anxiety. He has been having difficulties in his marriage and fears a dissolution in the near future.

Worrying about the future is a habit he has endured since childhood. He imagines the worst scenarios and attempts to resolve these possible future events by fantasizing solutions to them. He wants to make sure that if one does not work, he is ready to utilize a second and third choice of solution, thus assuring some form of security for himself … So at least he thinks! The truth is that he is in a constant state of preoccupation and suffering from anxiety, leading him to take medication for relief. In order to function at a calm level of energy at the clinic, he needs some help from the magic of tranquilizers. And tranquilized he is!

Alexander is so involved in his world of allopathic medicine that he does not stop to realize that he is trying to help others to calm down by means of explanation and talk, while he cannot stop his own anxiety without pills. Of course, he feels that his is a temporary anxiety brought about by his particular predicament. In his mind, he denies the many times in the past he was so anxious that he even contemplated suicide. While Alexander is in a healthier state of mind now (he no longer suffers from suicidal thoughts), he has not been able to *transcend* his often disquiet state of mind.

People are so used to worrying that they never question it, nor do they look at worry as anxiety. They go on suffering for years and years, believing they cannot do anything about it. Feeling trapped, they usually say, "That is the way I am." "I am a worrywart." "I can't help it." They very seldom consider their worrying as just fantasy. Indeed, in general we consider worrying a "given." We regard it as something to "put up with" and when it is unbearable we are quick to take a tranquilizer.

Because the brain does not distinguish between factual threats and imagined ones, they may produce the same level of anxiety in the organism. The flow of chemicals, the muscle tension needed in readiness for action are produced more or less equally in both cases.

We can enslave ourselves with belief systems; and we can curtail our rights to the freedom of being by believing our own fantasies. This is suffering!

A common source of anxiety is jealousy, which is mostly associated with phantasms of affairs, infidelities, and rejections. The latest television interview shows are full of programs addressing the pain, anger, and frustrations of jealousy. Observing the people being interviewed is an education in how people suffer due to the imagined affairs of their spouse or intimate friend. It is also an education in how *not* to live.

I use television as an example because it mirrors our prevailing trends and habits, and the paradigms of thinking in our society and humanity at large. Unfortunately these programs, watched by millions everyday, are not aimed at educating but at entertaining. It is true that most shows seem to have professionals (psychotherapists, psychiatrists, etc.) clarifying and making suggestions on "how to cope"; but their morsels of sophisticated knowledge are no more than the usual band-aids that have evolved from the same somnolent consciousness that brought about the problems in the first place. What we do not see being expressed is a commonsense way of looking at ourselves directly, in order to learn about ourselves and be totally responsible for an awareness of our way of functioning.

To wake up to our natural way of functioning is a blessing.

I encourage people to inquire, to look for themselves into the nature of thought, images, and fantasies. Worrying and anxiety, as well as their accompanying bodily changes, are made possible by our own natural way of psychophysical functioning in representations, memory, and images.

> *Have you ever looked at your own worrying?*
> *Have you noticed the content of thought during*
> *this special way of thinking?*

Some people believe they will always be anxious. They see themselves in their imaginations as nervous and anxious forever. They fantasize without being totally aware that they are making up stories in their minds. They negate all possibility of a reversal of whatever is going on with them at the time, or of a different approach to their predicament. Doctors reinforce this by prescribing medicine that acts fairly quickly, providing the quick fixes we have been conditioned to expect ever since the advent of analgesics like aspirin and tranquilizers like Valium. They often continue prescribing, without either checking the patients for a possibility of letting go of the medicine or encouraging them to be on their own. Unfortunately, doctors and patients are trapped in the same belief, *imagining* that it cannot be any other way. It is not necessary to suffer from anxiety; in the majority of cases it is not necessary to take pills to resolve it.

We need to be *fully aware*. And of course, we all want to know how to become "fully aware." There are hundreds or even thousands of books on this subject. If all the "how to's" that are available have not transformed or brought about transcendence of anxiety in humanity—and they most certainly have not—I do not see that another "how to" in this book could help anyone. Perhaps it might alleviate symptoms temporarily, just as medicine does, but there will be no *transcendence*.

Transcendence is a blessing we receive, rather than something we achieve through the pursuance of a goal, through a "how to." Unfortunately, we are so conditioned to accept someone else's instructions or belief about what we should do to heal ourselves or accomplish something, that we have lost our own wisdom in these matters.

My suggestion here is that the reader already knows how to transcend anything, and that all we can do here is simply talk about it. This is the honest approach to the truth of being human.

From ancient times meditation has been considered a powerful tool for transcendence, for full awareness or transformation. However, not everyone who meditates experiences or lives a transcended, fully aware, or transformed life. We cannot say that meditation automatically brings a radical change, since after more than five thousand years of meditation on the planet, humanity has yet to transform.

Nevertheless, meditation is very important; *it serves as an opportunity for an opening*. The time given to meditation is a relaxing time, also conducive to contemplation. It is an opportunity for insight, wisdom that changes the whole organism.

Since we have a rather fast-paced way of living, especially in the cities, it is important for our spiritupsychophysical health to spend time in total relaxation, in silence. Meditation is no longer the exclusive privilege of monastics or people involved in religion or esoteric beliefs. For some, to meditate is to simply sit quietly, to relax totally. For others, it is to experience peacefulness in daily living. Still to others, meditation is a religious or philosophical practice—a way of living. Today more physicians are recommending meditation, yoga, and guided imagery for relaxation to improve emotional or physical conditions. *Vipassana* is an excellent technique in which one practices awareness of what is happening to the body/mind in the moment of now. *Zazen* (Zen meditation) is a very old spiritual practice which can be of great benefit because of its focus on the moment—on "what is." Weekend or week-long silent retreats (whether religious or not) are also wonderful processes because they give an opportunity for neutral observation of mind-activity and the fantasizing qualities of the thought process. Such observation can bring home the truth of our busyness, our ambitious fantasies, and the consequent anxieties created in our society.

However, when the practice of any meditation is an activity done by rote, based only on a belief system without direct inquiry into one's own functioning, it may be no more than a relaxation period of lesser consequence. On the other hand, a genuine practice of silence twice a day may keep the doctor away!

Meditation may be most healing for anxiety sufferers who are living in an imagined doomed future, for in true meditative experience one lives the present. One cannot be anxious about a future event if one lives in the now.

11.

Sex and Fantasy

Sex is one of the greatest pleasures of human beings. It is also a source of suffering and moral confusion. While sex has been subject to taboo and liberal activity concomitantly, it has recently become less of a forbidden subject and more a "must talk about it and learn about it" topic on popular television shows.

That this is an era of sexual freedom is expressed and played like a broken record in commercials for everything from soap to tight jeans. Every product that can be associated with sex is promoted through the *sexy* image. Magazines, television, and newspapers carry advertisements filled with sexual innuendo and enticement.

"Sexiness" is continuously emphasized as one of a woman's most important qualities. The scanty burlesque costumes once condemned by mainstream society are today's fashion. Clothing for young people is advertised with the same sexy slant as adult wear. Thus, the image of the sexy woman is getting younger and younger. The fantasy is, "If you wear sexy clothing, you are in vogue, you will be liked, you will be important!" Given the fact that the majority of people (children and adults alike) watch television daily for hours on end, the commercials act to brainwash the masses.

The habitual fantasizing through so-called creative advertising continues to be unnoticed, as does the inculcation of fantasies about sexiness and its deleterious consequences. Novels and movies also greatly encourage fantasy. Furthermore, they often, overtly or covertly, guilefully portray sex as a destructive activity rather than the serious and beautiful intimate act of procreation that it actually is.

To many movie directors, explicit sex has become the only way to be realistic—realistic, that is, from the director's interpretation or point of view. Even movies rated PG (parental guidance) are becoming increasingly explicit, with the unintentional result of bringing specific *conditioning* to young and old alike. Images are very powerful; they remain in memory as models to be imitated. Thus one person's interpretation of sex becomes a "teaching" or an inculcation in the minds of viewers.

Young people are losing sight of the intimacy and beauty, the true meaning of sex. A good illustration of this is a young couple, both thirteen years old, who were taken to juvenile hall for performing sex in a department store. When interviewed and asked why they would pick such a place for their activity, they responded that "it was for the excitement of it." It seems as though young people do not find the sex act done in privacy exciting enough.

It is no different for adults. They also look for new and exciting ways to have sex. The use of fantasy for sex enhancement, from artifacts to pornographic magazines, videos, and movies, is an enormous business. These products dedicated to the promise of pleasurable sexual activity (directly or indirectly) also promote and perpetuate fantasy and habit. Let me give you some examples.

In my travels through India I met Lloyd, a fifty-six-year-old married man who was a follower of a well-known Indian guru. He was born in a culture where sex is included and depicted in religious and philosophical books; sexual acts are portrayed in sculpture on the façades of ancient temples. Part of the belief system, called Tantra, considers sex a path to spirituality. However, within Lloyd's family tradition sex was not a subject to be discussed. Marriages were arranged by the parents and pre-marital sex was out of the question. The culture and in particular the family mores in which Lloyd was raised had confusing messages.

From an early age Lloyd suffered from an obsession with sex. He needed pornographic pictures for his sexual fulfillment. At the same time, he felt that this curtailed his spiritual development. He felt that he had failed to obtain a spiritual path through Tantra and felt ashamed, guilty, and disappointed with himself. He had been married to his wife for many years. He occasionally had what he called an extramarital "fling" even though, as he said, "I love my wife. My parents picked the right bride, and I want to stay married to her. She is a great help to me."

These flings were rare and his obsession with sex had to be appeased mainly through self-stimulation and the use of pornographic materials. This mortified him because he considered such activity to be "beneath his dignity." He felt that he was on a "high spiritual path" and this obsession was a great obstacle to his "enlightenment."

If we were to deal psychologically with Lloyd's problem, we would begin to inquire into his past to find what incidents in his earlier life had caused the present behavior. Or we might look into the relationship between him and his wife: Was sex a problem in the marriage?

Since our approach is not through psychology, let us look at Lloyd from the point of view of the power of fantasy in human consciousness.

Fascination with sex was part of Lloyd's upbringing. As a matter of fact, his best friend and countryman, a politician, suffered from the same affliction. Talking with people in India disclosed to me their common conflict between spirituality and preoccupation with sex, or the "needs of the flesh," as it was expressed by one of the sufferers.

To complicate matters further, pornographic industries capitalize on the obsessions of individuals, perpetuating their predicament. The more creative the pornography, the more fantasies are encouraged in the minds of consumers. And, of course, the more revenue for the purveyors.

Lloyd and his friend looked for ways to end their predicament through psychotherapy as well as meditation, but to no avail. The more they sat in meditation the more the obsession about sex appeared. Eventually they realized that their practice of meditation was a learned activity, done by rote. It had become an attempt to escape from their problem, which eventually backfired. Finally, through intense, in-depth dialogue, they began to look at various factors that perpetuate obsession. They found this to be of most help to them. They were both highly intelligent, and the deep inquiry into their true nature, without a reliance on acquired knowledge, allowed their wisdom to unfold more fully. They returned to their meditation practices in a new way, questioning the dogma in order to understand more deeply their own spirituality.

At an experiential level, the main factors that they found were memory, fantasy, belief, and attachment. Let us look at these in more detail.

MEMORY. Remembering pleasure is an intricate and *reinforcing* element, creating a repetitive desire for sex. Thus for some individuals, the more memories of pleasure, the more fuel for desire. The mind becomes conditioned and habituated through the normal functions of memory. There has to be an innate, natural ability to become conditioned and habituated. *Obsessions are repetitious memory in action.* They are extreme preoccupation with or constant thinking of a particular subject.

FANTASY. The natural ability to abstract, make images, learn, and memorize plays an important part in sexual experiences; remembering previous pleasure facilitates the elaboration of an illusive sexual situation—a fantasy. Most people seem to use fantasy in their sexual activities. If this were not true, would we have industries dedicated to maintaining fantasy for sexual pleasure? Indeed, speaking with hundreds of people has revealed to me that this is a fact. It does not matter whether or not the person is "in love" with the sex partner, the fantasies are often secretly there, and may be a source of unexamined guilt.

BELIEF. At the moment of fantasy the whole organism responds as if whatever is in the mind is really happening. The fantasy is, at a somatic level, completely *believed* to be a real event. Masturbatory pleasure is based perhaps ninety percent on fantasy and ten percent on physical stimulation. Even though the person is cognizant that there is no one else outwardly participating, the fantasy is experienced inwardly as if a real person were there. The body systems involved in excitement (heart, sweat glands, etc.) tell the story. According to Dr. Jeanne Achtenberg, "fantasizing making love can lead to the same hormonal responses as the 'real' thing." As we have said in previous chapters, everything is representation to the brain. Therefore reality or imagination remain at the level of representation. Humans can experience sex and be just as emotional and pleasurably satisfied, whether the sexual act is with an actual person or with an imagined one. Outward and inward representations are images, and to the image maker, they are both "real."

ATTACHMENT. In addition to memory and belief, the attachment to pleasure and fantasy maintains the habitual and obsessive behavior. Furthermore, any accompanying guilt or shame brings about a depressed psychological state. To deal with the unhappiness, which individuals may interpret as being "sexually unfulfilled," they again seek the pleasure of fantasy to relieve their discomfort. In this manner a vicious cycle is established. Attachment, in this case to sexual desire, is an emotional movement in consciousness, giving the person a false sense of security. There is comfort in what is known, familiar, and there is fear of that which is unknown. Familiar fantasies and familiar pleasurable sensations may be a source of security, making attachment difficult to avoid.

There are people who say they "think about sex all day long." This was the case of Lloyd's friend. He complained that even though he had been involved in religious practices and teachings that explained consciousness as "maya," as illusion, it seemed to have done very little for his predicament.

Sex-obsessed sufferers are not truly aware that they are being dominated by an illusion, by habitual fantasy. They may be *cognizant* of the teachings about "illusion," they may understand them intellectually and be able to teach them to others; but there is no *full awareness* in their own movement of consciousness. There is no *transcendence* in their observation of the uncomfortable behavior. Therefore they continue to be habituated to fantasy/pleasure/pain.

Lloyd suffered from high blood pressure. His predicament was consequently alleviated by a medicine given to him which, according to physicians, tends to decrease libido. While the medicine could not completely eradicate his fantasy world of pornography, it gave him the chance to be more observant of himself. Eventually he was able to see, as he said, "the ridiculousness of the whole fantasy thing." He continued his meditation practices. Today he feels that his life is more integrated with his spiritual ideals, and he no longer suffers from the obsession.

Lloyd's friend was single when I met him, because he felt he "could not be loyal to one woman." The last time I heard from him he had left the political arena and was teaching, and in a letter from India expressed his gratefulness for the inquiries we had held in our brief dialogues. He continued to investigate fantasy, he said, and this had brought him to an awareness of human functioning he had not experienced before. He was happier and no longer obsessed with sex. He was presently involved in a relationship with a woman who he felt was, in his words, "truly fulfilling of spirit, body, and soul."

Today, the use of fantasy is accepted almost as a necessity for sexual arousal or for the enhancement of its pleasure. Via multiple workshops and popular talk shows on television, people are bombarded with information about sex and fantasy: the importance of sex; the many ways to use fantasy; the needed paraphernalia (sexy night gowns, massagers, etc.) to seduce or attract a mate; and even methods of attracting a "soul mate." Sex is good business these days!

Susan was beautiful (by American standards) and was "discovered" at a restaurant where waitresses "show more than food" to their customers. Now, she said, "I am able to put food on the table for my family and start up a marketing business of my own." She could also concentrate on her modeling career.

She was able to do all this through the magic of the "fantasy industry." Appearing in photographs on a sexy calendar and in an explicit sex video brought all the money she needed. Susan was very happy and never thought of the consequences that the video or alluring pictures might have on an emotionally unbalanced person or on young children, or the ongoing damage from fantasy to society at large. And why should she? She was applauded for her honesty, display of freedom, her "guts." Her fantasies of "making it in the world" had come true for her; why should she worry about anyone else? No one expected her to act differently, except those very strict people who condemn "lascivious" behavior. In her view, these people were entitled to their opinion. "Just don't dump a heap of guilt on me!" was her comment.

She is a product of our times, our paradigm of thinking:

"Dream your dream and do whatever it takes to make it happen."

"You have to think about yourself first."

"This is the nineties, the time of sexual freedom, the use of imagination, and the realization of dreams."

"We are not hurting anyone by our freedom. Besides, this is America!"

> *Have you heard these comments before? How do you react to all this? What are your views on fantasy and sex? This is for you to inquire into, rather than for me to give you a new set of beliefs.*

Even though we are somewhat free of the old sex taboos, the conditioning about propriety concerning sex is still very much in the general consciousness of human beings. In speaking with teenage children of prostitutes, I have rarely seen children who were not embarrassed about their mothers. Furthermore, children of women who are considered respectable housewives, but dress in a sexy manner, tend to be embarrassed by their mothers' appearance, sometimes to the point that they do not want to be seen with their mothers in public.

Some children may not have sex taboos themselves, except in relation to their parents. Often they express that they cannot imagine their parents having sex. Also, they do not like their parents' attempts to appear younger than their age by dressing like the younger generation. Parents behaving in this fashion are usually stuck in fantasies of being forever young and sexy.

Sex Abuse and Fantasy

Adults who molest children are emotionally infantile. Their behavior is not based on "what is," but on their fantastical distortion of reality. Their hearts are not touched by the pain they inflict on infants, children, or teenagers. They cannot feel for the other; they can only fulfill their own fantasies at any cost.

There is a pornographic industry catering to this rapidly spreading infantile behavior. Children are photographed in explicit sexual poses, and videos portraying sexual acts between adults and children are produced for the gratification of pedophiles, perpetuating pernicious fantasies in the consciousness of humanity.

These children, if they survive, will be tormented by their own memories of their past abuse. Psychotherapy can help sufferers to cope with and understand their pain, and in this there is alleviation. However, there may not be an eradication of the painful memories associated to fantasies linked to sexual pleasure. Let me elucidate.

Elda was a thirty-eight-year-old divorced woman with two married sons. She had been in psychotherapy for several years because of her memories of child abuse. She was still depressed, and now suffered from chronic fatigue syndrome. For three months she spent most of her time in bed, but with medication she was able to recuperate enough to be active and interested in the world again. When she came to dialogue with me, we agreed that this would not be a psychotherapeutic procedure;

all we could do would be to inquire into the nature of her human functioning.

After she related the story of her painful experiences, my first question to her was, "How do you feel now?" She answered, crying, "I feel terrible!"

My second question was, "Is all this happening to you now?"

"No!" she responded, puzzled.

"Well, then," I said, "why do you feel so terrible?"

"Because ... How would you feel if you had been abused as I was?" she said.

"I think I would have felt terrible *then*, at the time of the abuse," I responded, then continued, "Now, twenty years later, I would feel grateful and wonderful that I do not have to go through *that* again ... I imagine!"

"Oh?" she questioned.

"Do you like remembering your pain?" I asked.

"No, of course not; I just can't help thinking about it," was her reply.

And thinking about it, and thinking about it ... she did!

We began to inquire into thought and memory as natural functions. She understood that she could not change these natural processes. However, when we looked at the *contents* of thought and memory, she realized that she *could* do something about these, since they are not necessarily permanent.

Later we investigated the mind's fantasy *function*. Again, she could witness this as a natural process she could not change, for it is part of being human. As we further investigated the *content* of her fantasies, she came to comprehend deeply, through her own wisdom, *the impermanence of fantasy when there is no attachment* to its contents.

Eventually Elda realized that she was attached to repetitious fantasies of rape, which she had romanticized according to the novels she read. She had a passion for movies and novels, and she utilized these romantic fantasies to cope with her pain. She was, unawares, constantly remembering her past experience of abuse. This occurred through her romanticized fantasies, especially during sexual intercourse with a real or imagined partner.

The fantasies were keeping her on a merry-go-round of pleasure/ pain.

The human organism is capable of sexual pleasure (conscious or unconscious) while in pain, simply because sexual arousal is inevitable when there is nerve stimulation of the erotic zones. During rape or sexual abuse situations, this pleasure is not attended to, or it may not be noticed because it is overridden by the fear and the pain. Nevertheless it remains in the memory banks, suppressed or repressed.

This hidden natural pleasure is the source of much guilt and psychic pain because the victim is not supposed to enjoy in any way the assault on her body. Perhaps this is part of the reason many victims of rape may feel guilty, even though they know the rape was not their fault.

The person suffering from the memories of sexual abuse may have repetitious fantasies depicting a particular need for sexual pleasure, in a specific way and with a particular type of person. Fantasies very often hold the key to the healing process; but *full awareness* is needed. A person must be attentive to the *content* of the fantasies in order to take responsibility for this particular pleasure, as well as for possible unconscious attachment to the pleasure/pain cycles.

It is important for victims of abuse—as it is for all people—to take one hundred percent responsibility for their experience of all incidents in their lives. No matter whose fault an incident may be, we all are responsible for our subjective experience and interpretation of it. Being one hundred percent responsible is not an easy task. Each person must deeply understand his or her natural way of functioning, without judgment or evaluation.

In the case of sex abuse, the victim needs to understand experientially that:

1) pleasure of an erotic zone is natural, regardless of the circumstance;
2) the sensation or feeling that may have been experienced is not subject to morals, judgment, or evaluations;

3) pleasurable sensations are simple facts of the human body functions to be experienced just "as they are;"
4) the haunting fantasies (whether romanticized or not), as well as nightmares after sexual molestation, are also natural occurrences, *not* to be judged or evaluated;
5) attachment to fantasies and pleasure may be a consequence of trying to feel some security; it maintains the vicious circle of pleasure/pain.

Only insight or a full awareness of these things can bring about a transcendence in consciousness. All emotions, feelings, sensations and thoughts attached to the painful circumstances must be felt fully and totally, with awareness. This experience needs to include *seeing* the memories of the events, as well as the emotions accompanying them, *simply as memory*.

The person who takes full responsibility will be free from the phantasms of past memories of abuse and may enjoy the present life without self-blame and without hate for the perpetrators. The more *fully aware* abused people become, the more they are able to experience compassion for themselves and the aggressors. They may experience a life without guilt, and be able to have harmonious adult relationships.

Final Comments on Sex and Fantasy

Infantile sexuality is based solely on fantasy and pleasure. The choice of partner is not based on a natural expression of an innate drive, but on complex, conditioned preferences. The goal is realization of the fantasy pleasure.

Adult sexuality does not require fantasy. The partner is experienced exactly as he/she is, not fantasized as someone else. The pleasure is derived directly from the partner and from the natural excitement of erotic zones, and not from imagining other than "what is." Adult sexuality is a response to the natural urge to procreate.

Without fantasy, sex would simply be the original beautiful drive for procreation that it is, with sensations experienced as pleasurable. It would not be the conditioned societal obsession it has become. And it would not be a source of suffering!

12.

Fantasies in Society

As we have seen before, the imaginary line at Greenwich, England is the basis for the correct time all around the world. One could say that this imaginary line rules our schedules and, to a great extent, our way of living. We have agreed to be bound to time. We need to be "on time" for most things in this world today if we want to survive or if we want to have certain pleasures.

We must be on time for work; to board an airplane, a bus, train, or ship; concert or theater performances. One could go on and on …

We take all of these restrictions as normal, because we have agreed to maintain time for the sake of *order* in our world. This is commendable! What is of interest to me is that *order*, in this case, is being achieved through an *imaginary line* on the earth. In fact, this line may not be in the same relationship to the sun forever, because of the fluctuation in the rotation and position of the earth in relationship to the sun. Imagination is very powerful and, in this case, very useful!

I wish to point out, without judging or evaluating, our way of functioning; that is, that our imagination can be used constructively or destructively. An agreed upon system of time is necessary for transportation schedules, as well as for meeting someone, conducting business, and other orderly procedures in our society.

However, we can also use imagination destructively. For example when we look at the way we dress today, and the shoes that many women wear, we may see how destructive we can be. Spike heel shoes and short winter dresses are good examples of little concern for a healthy body.

We are ordinarily unaware that the fantasies of a few fashion designers influence societies. Of course, in the world of fashion this is called the couturier's or shoe designer's creativity. Given the inappropriateness and disregard for health of some fashions, one has to question if designers are truly creative or just fantasy-ridden human beings, competing to see who can be more famous or more "fantastique."

Actually, many couturiers themselves talk about "fantasy." They speak of creating an illusion for women "to feel good about themselves—beautiful and sexy." Unfortunately, women fall for the fantasy. Of course, they are not always perceived by others as beautiful or sexy while wearing the latest fashions, but they feel good because they are "in style," their dress and shoes are in "vogue."

This is the nature of societal consciousness. Consumers maintain the fantasies of producers, who in turn sustain the fantasies of the consumer. More merry-go-rounds!

> *What is your observation of all this? How do*
> *you view today's dress and shoe fashions? Do*
> *we dress according to what is healthy, or to*
> *impress others?*

Through the quantum leap in telecommunications and the aviation industry, entire societies are being influenced by the media. We can speak with another person thousands of miles away with the same ease with which we communicate with our next door neighbors. We can travel to the other side of the globe in just a few hours. We can buy and sell commodities around the world in minutes.

We all enjoy the advantages of the rapid mode of traveling and instant communication via satellites. At the same time these most beneficial, brilliant designs of technology carry the fantasies from one society to another on a grand scale. In earlier chapters we alluded to the influence of television, movies, and magazines. It does not matter what language is used or in which part of the world they are being produced, their end products look very much alike.

The female models in magazines are all thin. There is no difference, regardless of the country; all models must be thin or they do not get the top jobs. As a result, bulimia and anorexia nervosa are common afflictions among professionals and amateurs alike.

On the other hand, a new trend toward more curvaceous bodies is developing. Many women are having plastic surgery to augment their breasts, buttocks, or wherever more weight is needed for the emerging new image in the fantasy world of fashion.

All over the world, the enormous garment industry, as well as plastic surgeons, are being maintained and enriched by the consumer's illusions of beauty, sexiness, and wealth. Both creators and consumers of fantasy are unaware of the perils of their chimeras and their ensuing actions.

Many women are beginning to experience the deleterious consequences of plastic surgeries done for the sake of "glamour and sexiness," namely the use of silicone in the breasts, liposuction, and collagen on the face for wrinkles and pouty lips. After several years the silicone implants deteriorate and the solution begins to leak out. This is very injurious to women's bodies. Some women have complained of sagging of the skin in their faces where the collagen was injected. Others have sued their surgeons for "butchering" their faces or their bodies.

Some women even have surgery to make themselves look like "Barbie." The Barbie doll image has lasted for at least thirty years in the United States. In one extreme case, a woman had twenty surgeries in order to look like the famous doll. The fantasies start in childhood with the toys—guns or dolls—and continue to adulthood, without people realizing what is truly happening to them.

Societal consciousness approves of the realization of individual dreams. In America it is a cultural tradition to "follow your dream" and make it come true. In other words, do not give up your infantile fantasies, just make them come true.

We talk about the merits of individuality, but in fact we are more like sheep, blindly following the dictums of fashion and the conditioning fantasies. Our "followership" is comprised of our conditioned attitudes, beliefs, and actions which in turn contribute to the consciousness of our societies.

Another area in need of exploration is that of nutrition. There are restaurants in the United States that specialize in foods from different countries of the world. Part of the enchantment of these restaurants is the ambiance. They create the fantasy of the culture of the country they represent, and through this fantasy we enjoy the food and surroundings and say, *"Viva la differ-ence!"* Of course, we do not see that we may be ingesting food detrimental to our digestive systems, such as extreme amounts of fats and proteins that are very hard to digest. This is also occurring in other countries, where hamburgers and french fries, fried chicken, and many other fat-rich foods have become popularized through movie and television imagery.

Purveyors of beverages, too, sell their products via commercial fantasy. Television commercials for one of the large soft drink companies emphasize the "sexy" image fantasy. There is no mention of the sugar, caffeine, and other ingredients that are hazardous to the health when consumed in excess, as many Americans do. Coffee commercials create the fantasy of a relaxing time with a full cup of coffee in hand; or waking up to the aroma of a cup of coffee that will invigorate you for the rest of the day. Actually coffee makes many people nervous, and is very addictive.

In the sense of double messages, the most hypocritical advertisement is the beer company commercial advising people to help those who over-drink by driving them home or calling for someone else to drive. The image of the "good person" getting a taxi to help an inebriated one, detracts from the real danger of overindulgence. The tacit implication is that it is all right to

drink in excess, as long as someone else drives; thus we perpetuate the fantasy that "it is all right to get drunk." The beer company people are not concerned with the catastrophic
consequences of overuse of their product. They are concerned
with their own image, and through the illusion-weaving
commercials make themselves out to be "good guys." It is all
fantasy!!

In the meantime, liquor is part of the teenager's fantasy of fun
partying (just as it is illustrated in the advertisements). The illusion of being part of the "gang of drinking buddies" obliterates
the reality of accidents, addiction and unhappiness in themselves and their families.

The fantasy world of novels, television, and the movies contributes to deleterious movements in our consciousness. The
fantasy of violence sells very well in our society. Movies make
millions of dollars for the producers, directors, and the "stars."

Movies are full of fiery explosions, accidents, killings, and
guns, guns, guns! Killing has been romanticized from the very
beginning of the movie era. "Cowboys and Indians" movies
were perhaps the beginning of our romance with guns. Today,
the romance is with powerful assault weapons.

The fantasy of guns begins very early in the life of the child.
We have a large assortment of toy guns for children to choose
from. Whatever they see being used in the movies is what they
want—the Ninja Turtle's gun or the machine gun of a Rambo,
and so on …

Past and future wars have also been romanticized through
movies like *Gone with the Wind* and *Star Wars*. Movies like *Star
Wars* become imprinted in the minds of young people and in
turn serve as a basis for their imagination of the future—the
kinds of airplanes and weapons they can invent.

In our society, people have been enriched by the proliferation
of deadly weapons. Individuals, as well as our government,
profit from this industry. As a society we depend on guns,
bombs, and nuclear weaponry for national security. We want
armaments as a deterrent, rather than meaningful dialogue
with other nations. We create attitudes and beliefs that develop

mind-sets in consciousness. Every society has cultivated mind-sets, such as the fear of other nations' weapons; they in turn accumulate their own arsenals to make sure they are not swallowed up by larger or more powerfully armed countries. It is the representations, or what I call in this book *fantasy*, that formulate our reality. At present, our reality is shaped by the belief in nuclear power for our national protection—a belief which, in fact, threatens to devastate the planet. *Protection through nuclear weaponry is our greatest survival fantasy.* Nevertheless, it is all very rational to us. We have been reasoning violence from time immemorial. Through the rationalization of self-defense in wars, the image of the hero, in actuality as in movies, has been praised and romanticized, while the truth of the actual killing of another human being has been minimized.

We have reasoned and justified that for "self-defense" the killing of thousands of people with two atomic bombs was necessary, while it was "evil" to kill millions of people in gas chambers for an ideal of a "better world." This I consider the fantasy world of a blind consciousness negating the actuality of innocent children and adults alike being slaughtered or maimed. If we continue to support our self-centered way of thinking and accept such rationalizations, we will continue to destroy each other and the planet.

I have to question: Is our rationality a product of our own representations? our fantasies? Is it an elaborate way of thinking that is based on self-centered needs and propagated through acculturation? Each one of us contributes to the whole by the way that we raise and educate our children. Each one of us contributes to the consciousness of humanity with our own thinking mode and its consequent actions. We are intimately interrelated members of the whole of humanity. We are like the parts of a clock; when all are sound the clock works perfectly; but when one is damaged, the clock will malfunction.

We are not experientially aware of our total interrelatedness; therefore, we do not see our own way of thinking and acting to be intimately related to the present state of humanity. It is for this reason that we have not, *individually*, come to experience our responsibility for humanity as a whole. We have to understand with full awareness, our oneness, and see that each one of us, like an integral part of the clock, is responsible for the perfect functioning, the well-being of the whole.

Oneness as a *concept* is easy to understand, but remains a mind-fantasy. Oneness as a *way of living* is the truth of our interrelated existence. It is for this reason that I want to emphasize that we need to live this *truth* of our oneness, not the *fantasy* of it, and that it is up to each individual to be responsible for the whole of humanity.

Traditions also are a very important element in the perpetuation of culture. Most people want and enjoy traditions.

The word *tradition* in Webster's New World Dictionary represents:

a) "the handing down orally of stories, beliefs, customs, etc. from generation to generation; a story, belief, custom, proverb, etc., handed down this way;"

b) "a long established custom or practice that has the effect of an unwritten law; specifically any of the usages of a school of art or literature handed down through the generations and generally observed."

Traditions are originally based on memory kept alive through verbal transmission. Most of the present religious belief systems began through oral communications and were established through the written word only after many years.

Orally transmitted folk tales, stories, proverbs, beliefs, and so on are held in the memory and transmitted through the imagination of the person entrusted with specific rituals or religious practices—shaman, medicine person, elder teacher, or simply parents. As these oral transmissions pass through generations some become customs or practices that carry with them the "effect of an unwritten law."

Given the way our imaginations work, the original stories change with time, and what remains is the root of the custom. For example, the celebration of Christmas, while having its origin in Christianity, is celebrated somewhat differently in different countries. In Uruguay where I was born, there was no tree in the house and no gifts brought by Santa Claus as in the typical celebration in the United States. The religious practices of Christmas are very similar since the church celebrations are based on the written form of the tradition, the Bible. But the rest of the festivities are different. The children receive the gifts on the sixth of January, commemorating the day the three Kings (Magos or "magic kings" in Uruguay) arrived, bringing gifts for baby Jesus. However, the *traditional fantasy* created for the young, namely the expectation of gifts, remains the same … and so remain the many disappointments that children endure through these well-established customs in both countries.

Fantasy is encouraged from an early age in society through tradition, and maintained in consciousness through the many ramifications the customs create. Customs, beliefs, which are representations in the mind, are powerful conditioning tools.

Each culture has mores, standards, prejudices, superstitions, beliefs, rules, and laws which constitute its paradigm of thinking. All of these are acquired and passed on from generation to generation through the traditional modes of communication of each particular society, and they manifest in the language and behavior of people. The members follow a lifestyle which is dictated by the conditioning power of the particular paradigm of thinking of the society. It is in this manner that we establish our agreed-upon reality.

Traditions can also serve as a basis for new approaches. For example, shamanism and Native American cultural rituals are very popular these days, and very much a part of the New Age movement. The use of drums, rattles, and other paraphernalia, together with the use of imagination may, in time, become a combined tradition; a new belief system.

Final Comments

Actually, fantasies are very important in our society. Through them we maintain:

- commercialism;
- life styles;
- dressing styles;
- eating and drinking habits;
- costumes/traditions.

> *Have you ever asked yourself, if we did not*
> *attend or practice the dictums of societal fantasy,*
> *could we survive?*

I would like to end the chapter with this question, because it seems vital that we inquire into our habits, lifestyles, state of health, and so on. We need to question our gullibility and tendency to follow the crowd.

Inquiring into the truth of all this may bring you to a transcendent awareness of yourself and your own society.

13.

Fantasy, Health, and Imagination

*"There is a part of the mind that we don't really
know about and it is that part that is most
important in whether we become sick or remain
well."—Thomas Largewhiskers, 100-year-old
Navaho medicine man*

These words of Thomas Largewhiskers are as true today as ever; we are not fully aware of the mind's potential for propitious as well as ruinous effects. The mind is the most powerful known aspect of humankind. It brings about happiness or unhappiness, health or illness, simple peaceful living or complex stressful living, joy or suffering. When the limitations of the life of opposites in the mind are dissolved, the fully aware (awakened) person experiences life completely and joyfully.

Let us now look into the destructive fantasies that create unhealthy living and the constructive imagery that brings about healing.

Disease and Fantasy

She was fifty-five years old and suffered from juvenile diabetes. This is a pernicious disease that starts very early in life, and demands great fortitude to deal with, great faith to overcome.

Julie was unfortunately not strong in her resolutions to manage the debilitating disease. She "knew" it was going to kill her at an early age.

Julie believed she had a right to be fulfilled and to enjoy her body. Instead of maintaining a strict diet to manage the diabetes, she often ate to satisfy her taste for sweets and fats. She would indulge for a while and then go on her needed diet for a time. She repeated this pattern for years while also taking insulin. Even though she was cognizant of the consequences, she continued to fantasize that her indulgence was all right because she always went back to her diet.

She carried in her mind a fantasy of how she would become progressively worse. She had learned all about diabetes, and the pattern of this dreadful disease was happening in her just as she thought it would. Whenever anyone mentioned the possibility of remission, she would say, "I know it is possible with some illnesses, but you do not know what it is to have this problem. Just read the scientific evidence and you will see that I do not have much of a chance, no matter what!" Usually after saying this her facial expression would become solemn, like that of a martyr, as depicted in novels and movies.

This certainty of doom in her mind always astonished me. There was no space in her whole being for remission or miracles, even though she recognized them intellectually as possibilities; but she insisted that her case was different. From an early age she had heard about her plight from allopathic doctors who also believed in the doom of diabetic "victims." As a matter of fact, it is not unusual to read or hear the expression, "victim of the disease." This expression reflects a powerful attitude, intrusively pervading consciousness today, that is becoming a general mind-set. It denies the power of remission and the natural healing ability of the sufferer's mind.

Julie was always imagining a future with her beloved, a married man, whom she waited for years to be divorced. She knew he would be "devastated" by her death, she confided. She knew "he would be sorry" they had not gotten together. She was very much in love!

One has to question to what extent her fantasies and mind-sets contributed to an early death. She often ignored the actuality of her body's weakness by fantasizing a superficial healthiness, causing her not to follow the dietary regime her body required. "It is too hard. I want to enjoy life, and I like having a glass of wine and ice-cream and chocolates whenever I want to!" was her complaint regarding her diet. Julie did not live the truth of her body's condition. She lived in a fantasy world of opposites. When she felt strong and healthy she thought, "I'm okay. I can eat anything I want." But when she felt weak and diseased she would say, "I will slowly deteriorate and no one can do anything about it."

She actually felt she was always being realistic about her illness. However, when approached with alternatives and possibilities of healing by attending strictly to her diet and mind-sets, the resistance permeated her reasoning and justifications. She superficially experimented with healing alternatives such as "spiritual healers," guided meditations, and prayer, but to no avail. "I will try, but I don't want to fool myself," she would say. While this was realistic from an allopathic diagnostic view that claims no cure, she lacked the determination of spirit to really explore and discover all possibilities.

Finally the day came when Julie had to face the fact that her body was not responding well. She was losing ground, so she needed to take different measures. "I am dying, but I am prepared. I always knew I had to die young." And prepared she was, from leaving a will, to the plans for her funeral. It was a romantic funeral, with poetry and song. She had fantasized these services many times. She had gone over in her mind the responses people would have when she died. About the funeral her son said, "She certainly orchestrated it well! That was Julie, always the director!"

It is not unusual for people to fantasize and romanticize their funeral. Romantic sufferers take pride in their attitude about death, especially when everyone around them is fearful. They are heroes or heroines in their own eyes.

Making plans for one's funeral and burial is not the same as romantically fantasizing about it. Once the plans are made, the subject is dropped and no longer a concern. In our society this is considered a healthy approach to the inevitable event. However, the romanticization of death and funerals is in the realm of fantasy, and therefore a stimulus for unhealthy, dispiriting thinking patterns. Instead of being fully alive, the person is half-dead through fantasy.

Furthermore, these ways of thinking become paradigms in consciousness, perpetuated through cinema and television. *Camille*, one of the classics portraying the romantic death of a heroine afflicted with a deadly disease, has been played over and over in novels, plays, and movies and on television screens.

Addictions and Fantasy

One of the most pervasive, illusory ways of thinking is among heavy smokers. They are under the illusion that they will not be affected by cigarettes. After all, "George Burns has smoked cigars all his life, and look at him. He is very much alive and almost a hundred years old! I too could live to be a hundred." I have heard this rationalization many times.

We can no longer reason that it takes education to maintain a healthy society. We have plenty of research and education on the subject of smoking; yet people keep smoking and dying of lung cancer, emphysema, and heart disease.

The same can be said regarding alcohol. Education has made little difference in the number of accidents caused by drunk drivers. Alcoholics continue to kill themselves and others on the highways. They batter and abuse adults and children alike. We have plenty of knowledge and experience of the devastating effects of alcohol, but people continue to overindulge and die of cirrhosis of the liver and other alcohol-related diseases.

"Oh! I know I can quit, I have done it before!" is the illusory assurance made by people addicted to alcohol. Drug addicts have a similar attitude to alcoholics; most addicts live in a fantasy world of "I can quit at any time, and I will!" ... but, of course, "not right now." Still others fall into a belief in the fantasy "I cannot quit, no matter what I do!"

Among people who are overweight, the most damaging *believed* fantasy is, "I don't want to be fat." I am talking here of people who have checked with a medical doctor and are in good health with no glandular conditions or diseases. They are certain they want to lose pounds. When questioned about what they truly want, most people do not know how to respond. Let us look at a conversation typical of those I have had with many overweight people.

Person: "I am so tired of diets. I have tried and tried but it is no use. Every time I stop dieting I gain what I lost and more!"

Ligia: "Are you on a diet now?"

Person: "Well, sort of. I am always on a diet of some kind."

Ligia: "Are you on a strict diet?"

Person: "No, not now. I really have to do something."

Ligia: "Do you want to be fat?"

Person: "No!"

Ligia: "Is that your body?"

Person: "Of course it is."

Ligia: "If you do not want to be fat, who does?"

Person: "Well I don't know; but I certainly don't want to be fat!"

Ligia: "If this is your body and it is fat, who is feeding it?"

Person: "Well, I am, but I don't want to gain weight."

Ligia: "Who is gaining the weight?"

Person: "I am. But I do not want to."

Ligia: "If this is your body and you are gaining weight, who wants to gain weight?"

Person: "I don't know. I can assure you, I do not want to be this heavy."

Ligia: "Who puts the food in your mouth?" ... and so on ...

While this kind of inquiry is done very gently, it is actually very confronting and not easy to go through. Most people will not admit their responsibility for their weight; therefore they continue to be in denial.

To compound the problem of denial, advertisements for

weight reduction clinics proclaim, "It is not your fault." This claim gives the opportunity for addicted persons to fantasize about being victims of something beyond their control.

Overeating and over-drinking are considered *diseases* and the sufferers the victims of the disease. The treatment is according to the diagnosis of disease; the clinicians, of course, have *the cure*.

There seems to be a lack of actuality to this reasoning. While people are treated as having an illness, they can fantasize about not being responsible for overindulgence of alcohol or food. After all, it is "not their fault" that they overdo it. Such advertisements are too often designed to entice more clients to the clinics. Since the general public is already conditioned to go to doctors for ailments, they make it easier for the sufferer to come by saying, "It is not your fault; you have a disease."

For many people there is no embarrassment about being ill, while they would find it shameful to go to Alcoholics Anonymous or Overeaters Anonymous. Taking that step is harder for some people because they have to be responsible and "tell it like it is." They must admit they are alcoholics or addicts and take responsibility for their lives. Even though this step is more difficult, it is actually very beneficial. The admission of addiction prevents fantasizing that they have an ailment caused by extraneous circumstances over which they have no control. People can acknowledge that they are responsible for what they put in their mouth every moment of the day regardless of the reasons for their dilemma.

Recently, some researchers have found a specific gene in overweight people. This discovery has an unfortunate side effect; obese people begin to use the facts as excuses. I have heard people say that they cannot help but be overweight because "It is in my genes. It is inevitable, I will always be overweight." They seem to think that there is no solution to obesity. However, if they simply open their eyes and see that they are using this reasoning as an excuse to indulge, they can find the specific nutrients that their body requires to maintain a healthy weight for the well-being of their entire organism.

The facts discovered by scientific research help some obese

people to elaborate a reverie of doom about their body. "It is always going to be this way," or, "I am always going to be fat." This way of thinking actually remains as a fantasy, preventing the person from inquiring into nutrition and the types of food that would be appropriate for the structure of their body. In other words, if the person has a gene that tells the organism to make fat at a greater rate than the average, then whatever the person eats must be carefully calculated to compensate for the particular message from the "fat-gene."

It takes dedication, patience, and above all constancy to learn all the facts regarding one's obesity and then follow through by *eating appropriately for a lifetime*. For example, supposing that there is a particular congenital defect in the metabolizing process of the body, the person needs to find out what kinds of food are going to be assimilated without making fat. For some people it may be necessary to stay away from complex carbohydrates or certain proteins for the rest of their life. Unfortunately, the conditioned desire of most people for fats, sugars, and processed foods is stronger than their desire for a healthy body and healthy living. They would rather fantasize that they can lose weight and eat what they crave, than face the facts that the kind of foods they need to eat for the rest of their lives may not include any of the foods they love.

There has to be unison within all aspects of our Spiritupsychophysicalness. There has to be an alignment within the realms of mind/body. Therefore, if we want to live a healthy life, the most crucial factor is *full awareness*. If our behavior is going to depend solely on our conditioned thinking, our fantasy world, we will continue to exist in a somnolent consciousness, a consciousness based on a vicious circle of pleasure/pain. We need to wake up and be responsible for ourselves.

The Mind/Body Function

We have been looking at the deleterious aspects of fantasy in disease and addiction. Let us now look at the beneficial use of imagination—which is also fantasy as we have delineated it in this book.

The idea of mind over matter is not new. Many books have been written on the subject. There are hundreds of workshops, seminars, and audio tape programs on the market teaching how to use your mind to heal yourself. There are religions such as Science of Mind in which some teachers emphasize the use of mind for everything from healing to being wealthy.

Researchers have found how powerful the relationship is between the psychological and physiological aspects of the human organism. In studies of cases of multiple personalities they have discovered a correlation between physiological activity and the different corresponding personalities. In one particular case the person was a diabetic when one of the personalities was in consciousness, but the disease disappeared when another personality took over. In another case, a young man suffered from allergies; he was allergic to orange juice in one personality but had absolutely no reaction to the juice in another personality.

Furthermore, there is a new developing science called psychoneuroimmunology, which is a direct study of the interrelationship of the immune, endocrine, and neurological systems. In recent years scientists have discovered the direct relationship of the brain and the immune system. But they also know that there is a life energy that goes beyond their findings.

Scientist Candace Pert expressed this clearly in an interview with Bill Moyers when she said, "The mind is some kind of an enlivening energy in the information realm throughout the brain and the body that enables the cells to talk to each other, and the outside to talk to the whole organism."

The body/mind connection is no longer an issue in scientific medical arenas. The traditionally believed separation between them remains only as a persistent residual attitude in consciousness today. The younger physicians seem to acknowledge and deal more often than their predecessors with the psychosomatic nature of illness. Some physicians take time to talk to their patients about their family situations or their stress, rather than just treating their symptoms and sending them home. Some hospitals allow visitors at any time of the day because it actually helps the patient psychologically. Many maternity wards have changed drastically. The husband is encouraged to be present at the delivery and is able to stay overnight in the same room with the wife, this being considered very effective for the mother/father/baby bonding process.

Today many health professionals advocate the use of the mind for healing. The use of imagination, visualizations, guided meditations, prayer, and maintaining a positive attitude is becoming more widespread. Yoga and meditation are being suggested for relaxation and health as well as for spiritual expression. Some insurance companies pay for alternative medical clinics that use these techniques. Until a few years ago this was not accepted, but today physicians like Dean Ornish have gained the respect of insurance companies. Dr. Ornish has had much success with his patients using guided meditation, yoga, and deep relaxation as an important part of his program for reversing heart disease.

Constructive Use of Imagination

"The word 'health' itself is so interesting
because it comes from a root that means 'whole.'
Part of being a healthy person is being well
integrated and at peace, with all of the systems
acting together."—Candace Pert

According to Candace Pert, to be healthy is to be whole. At a global level, given the divided, conditioned mode of thinking of most human beings, there is not much of a chance for humanity as a whole to experience health. In general, human thought processes are not truly aligned with wholeness. If we were truly aligned with wholeness we would be very concerned with the kinds of food we produce, the kind of environment we live in, the kinds of arsenals we have, the kinds of cars and airplanes we build, and how much of the natural resources we use without polluting and devastating the planet.

At the individual level, our divided way of living is definitely not conducive to real health. We live as separate units involved in self-centered behavior based on our conditioned likes and dislikes, family traditions, and societal mandates. In general, we tend to follow the latest trends instead of investigating healthy ways of eating and dressing. For example, we consume more prepared foods than fresh foods such as vegetables and fruits.

We blindly accept medical treatments using drugs that have dangerous side effects, without examining alternative medicinal herbs. Furthermore, we neglect to inquire about and discover the real potential of our own body/mind healing wisdom.

As Ms. Pert says, part of being a healthy person is being whole, *integral*. Thus we need to be aware of our own lack of integrity. By integrity I do not mean a moralistic attitude, but a quality or state of being complete, whole, undivided, having all aspects of our humanness working in unison. In other words, spirit/mind/body or spiritupsychophysicalness is experienced as interrelated processes and not separate parts independently functioning. It is for this reason that we need to address the use of fantasy in healing. Since representation (fantasy/imagination) is a normal activity of mind function, we now want to investigate its constructive potential.

The body responds physiologically, whether we imagine something (inner stimulus) or we perceive something through the senses (outer stimulus). Our blood pressure may rise just as surely by thinking about something unpleasant as by having an argument with someone. In her book *Imagery and Healing*, Dr. Jeanne Achtenberg points out that "Imaging noxious stimuli have been associated with physiological arousal as measured by heart rate, muscle tension, and skin resistance levels." These kinds of arousals can also be measured in real situations, upon direct perceptions through the senses.

The fact that imagination affects our whole organism is important in relation to fantasy; first, because we must be aware of how we can become ill through negative fantasies; and second, because we can also heal ourselves by the use of imagination. *The use of fantasy (imagination) in the context of healing is greatly beneficial.* The literature is replete with ways to use the imagination for healing.

The following are some examples:

1) A relaxation routine, followed by imagining the afflicted area being bathed in white or pink light that is healing that area completely.
2) A relaxation routine, followed by imagining oneself sitting in the center of a beautiful red rose, engulfed by its beauty and fragrance, experiencing its healing power.
3) A relaxation routine, followed by imagining the immune system cells of one's body engulfing the malignant cells of cancer, as well as viruses.
4) A relaxation routine, followed by imagining the heart chakra expanding through the entire body.

The human body is constantly repairing itself. Immediately after an injury or the onset of an infection or illness, the organism automatically responds with its immune system's repairing and curative procedures. This occurs faster than we can think; before we are cognizant of any physical disarray, we are already healing ourselves. To assist this process we need awareness and a way of thinking that *aligns* with the natural healing process already freely flowing like a bubbling brook.

While the healing is an actuality, we are not cognizant of the incredibly swift action of the cells, organs, and body chemistry. We are least cognizant of the activity at the molecular and subatomic levels. The marvel of healing is too fast for our thinking process to fathom, but we can sort of "catch up" by imagining the curative process.

When we think about the body chemistry—the many cells, organs, and molecular structures involved in the healing process—we begin to experience the truth of our functioning bodies.

We begin to feel our quantum quality. By this I mean that we may experience being the discrete bundles of energy (quantum) we truly are. When we experience ourselves as energy, we are in unison and not separate from *what is*. So when we are ill, instead of fantasizing about how much worse we can get or what can happen to us, weaving some sentimental or morbid scenario, we have the opportunity to use the mind's natural ability to fantasize and imagine how the body is healing itself.

My personal approach to guided imagery for healing is always related to the truth of our body's wisdom. Rather than focusing on more indirect visualization techniques, I prefer to emphasize *aligning the thought process with the healing process that is already occurring in the body.*

After a deep relaxation routine where I ask people to be conscious of their entire bodies by going through them slowly in their minds, from toes to face, I begin the guided meditation by asking them to visualize all of the internal organs, aligning and working in unison with the cells of the immune system to heal the disease or the particular area of concern; to experience their existence in space where the power of creation reigns, and where all possibilities exist. I usually end the guided meditation by asking them to see themselves in perspective with the universe and to experience themselves as the universal energy they are.

Laying on of Hands

The laying on of hands for healing is an ancient practice. Today, however, the use of imagination coupled with this old ritual has become another lucrative business. The art of healing has been a tradition passed on from generation to generation by the shaman, the curandero, or the medicine man. Today, schools have been established to teach "How to heal others" through guided imagery and the laying on of hands. Again, fantasy or imagination is a coveted tool.

Fantasy is a natural function of our thought process, rapidly being capitalized upon by people who are more concerned with personal profit than the well-being of humanity as a whole. We need to be aware of how we can be seduced by the new trends and be caught in a New Age conditioning fad.

As we have seen, the use of imagination, fantasy, can be very constructive when it is a spontaneous alignment of the thought process with the natural healing processes of the organism. It is not constructive or helpful when it is used for the sole purpose of personal profit.

Several years ago a mother came to talk with me, complaining that she could not truly heal herself like she had in the past. This woman had learned techniques for healing from one of the most popular schools, but they were now failing her "miserably."

She had gone to school for a long time and she felt she was a healer. She had felt the heat in her hands and she had dreamed of a healing practice and being a famous healer of this century.

"But you are telling me that the techniques are failing you," I proceeded.

"Well, maybe it is me. I am failing! Maybe I am not the healer I thought I was."

She had embarked on a fantasy of being a famous healer, encouraged by the teachers in her New Age school that taught healing by the laying on of hands. She was totally disappointed and wondered how she could regain the healing power she felt before. Since the feelings of healing power she felt were apparently part of the weave of her fantasies, her dreams of being famous, she had to face the actuality of her predicament, the fact that the "way it is" was very different than her fantasies. She had to let the fantasies go, and began to put in perspective the value of what she called "New Age beliefs" about healing, and the truth of the natural process.

I have heard variations of this story several times. People become quite disillusioned with the promises of healing powers. It takes them a while to realize and admit that they have been caught in a belief system and fantasy, and not at all in touch with the healing powers of the organism's innate spiritual energy.

Spontaneous Remissions/Miracle Cures

Physicians have long been perplexed by the phenomenon of spontaneous remission. They cannot, to this day, explain how it occurs; they can only acknowledge that it happens and that it is rare. Let me relate to you a very interesting case my friend Dr. Miller witnessed. The patient had a tumor that could clearly be seen on the x-rays, apparently attached to the esophagus. The decision was made to operate. The morning of the surgery more x-rays were ordered and a fluoroscopy procedure was used to pinpoint the site of the incision. Everything was ready, the nurses and doctors around the surgical table, the patient sedated. As the surgeon pressed the appropriate levers to turn on the fluoroscopy to view the inside of the patient's body, there was a problem: the tumor could not be seen. The doctors turned their attention to the x-rays that had been taken that morning and the tumor was there, as clear as could be! How could this happen? Was there something wrong with the fluoroscopy machine? Was this a special type of tumor invisible through this particular light? The doctors were totally perplexed and very concerned as to what to do. After serious consideration they opted for performing the surgery, thinking that the failure to see the tumor was in the machine itself.

The incision was made at the position of the tumor according to the films taken that morning, but it was not there. They made sure that it had not shifted … Finally they realized that, indeed, there was no tumor to be found. How could it have disappeared? There was no evidence of fluid or debris suggesting that something extraneous to the organism might have been there. The esophagus area was normal and healthy. They closed the incision and sent the patient back to his room after the necessary time for recovery from the anesthetic. Dr. Miller had seen patients recover miraculously many times before, but never had he witnessed a case of such spontaneous remission. It was the talk of the day at the hospital. Then, the patient called this an act of malpractice and sued Dr. Miller and the other surgeon for opening the chest after they had seen in the fluoro-scope that the tumor was not there.

It is difficult for a conditioned mind to think in terms of mira-cles. The doctors could not believe that an organism could heal itself in the way this patient's did. The truth is that the wisdom of the body is infinite and we have not fathomed its power. When we use fantasy, guided imagery, for healing we are actually aligning the thought process with this kind of infinite power.

Summary

Fantasies are destructive to health when:

a) fantasy takes the form of negative memories of past experi-ences in relationship to health;
b) beliefs of possible doom are held as mind-sets, disallowing the possibility of natural, spontaneous healing;
c) a person negates responsibility by fantasizing that the health problem is due to external circumstances or caused by others;
d) the disease is romanticized.

Fantasy is constructive when:

a) it is used in relaxation techniques or guided meditations;
b) the content of the imagining brings the thought process into alignment with the natural healing power of the organism.

14.
Spirituality, Transitions, and Fantasy

We are quantum beings, creation itself. The true experience of this without belief or fantasy is an experience beyond ordinary consciousness.

In previous chapters we talked about the intimate and inseparable activity of body/mind; but we have not yet talked about the third aspect—spirit. Spirit does not have a generally agreed-upon reality like a rose, an object, or time, a concept everyone all over the world accepts. Instead, it is deemed a religious matter. Spirit is often used synonymously with God, the Divine, Soul, the Supernatural, that which cannot be demonstrated or perceived directly by the senses.

To the atheist or the materialist, spirit is a fantasy, a figment of the mind or an attempt to explain out of the ordinary experiences, the paranormal, or the unknown. Given our propensity to fantasize, perhaps much of our understanding of the word *spirit* may be involved in fantasy rather than direct existential human experiences.

I am referring to the word *spirit* here as it is represented in one of the dictionary definitions: "The thinking, motivating, feeling part of man often as distinguished from the body; mind; intelligence." I am not using the word *spirit* to represent an entity inside or outside of the human body, nor do I intend to use it as it is proposed by any religious or philosophical belief.

Spirit is a concept intrinsic to religion. Most religions depended on the oral transmission of their beliefs until the written form became available. Since we have an ability mentally to elaborate (imagine, fantasize) and symbolize, religious teachings may have gone through many changes through the years before they were written down, and different symbols may have been added as others have been dropped. We cannot determine with certainty how much of what was related through religious beliefs is factual and how much is imagination.

It has been my observation that in the last thirty years or so, religions as well as what is called spirituality have been going through a definite change. I have witnessed some churches giving up many traditions and replacing them with more up to date activities (such as modern music rather than traditional hymns and new types of sermons and services). Televangelism is certainly a very different approach to religion. Some of it is closer to entertainment than traditional evangelism. It seems to have adopted the imaginative/fantasy modality of television.

There also seems to be a New Age spirituality that is generally considered to have started with the youth revolution of the sixties: sexual freedom, psychedelic drugs, the human potential movement, and the revival of American Indian cultures. Associated with these movements are alternative healing practices such as shamanism and the laying on of hands. Furthermore, Eastern religious practices such as yoga, Buddhism, and Zen meditation have been popularized as part of the New Age consciousness.

Beliefs in reincarnation, past lives, kundalini, and chakras have been incorporated into New Age spirituality. There are hundreds of New Age teachers all over the world serving as exponents of the old beliefs but with different, modern explanations.

For example, Dr. Deepak Chopra has combined contemporary medical theories with old Ayurvedic beliefs and processes in a New Age approach to health care which he says is very spiritual. Indeed, he acknowledges the power of spirit at the same time that he bases many of his explanations on quantum physics theory.

The new-old approaches to healing have brought about conflict in some practitioners. They vacillate between conditioned thoughts of the more traditional spiritual healing practices, which are done for free, and the practice of providing services for a fee, typically done in allopathic medicine.

Some practitioners have shared with me the conflict they experience regarding their work as counselors or spiritual healers. They struggle between their natural, heartfelt spiritual feelings to do the work for free and their need to charge in order to survive. They are usually in a quandary that can only be resolved when their conditioned attitudes or their ambitious fantasies (conscious or unconscious) for wealth and power are given up; this is a shift in consciousness. That is, their spirituality and what they do in life are no longer separated by the need to survive through a *certain style of living*. Mother Teresa is a quintessential example of total dedication to spiritual healing without concern for more than the essentials for survival. Of course she is one of the unusual beings in this planet, serving humanity.

Many healers and spiritual counselors (most of whom include the use of imagination in their work) have achieved financial success. As a matter of fact, some practitioners seem to have more of a business than a spiritual practice. The New Age seems to me to be simply more of the Old Age with new twists, with purveyors being led by the same illusions or fantasies of wealth and aggrandizement that are typical of our society. Many more hopefuls are still dreaming the American dream of "achievement" that these new gurus of healing spirituality represent, thus filling the many classes offered on "spiritual healing."

Modern spirituality seems to keep some people stuck in new conditioning and fantasies, as well as to bring a certain amount of disillusionment to many. Let me give some illustrations.

Many years ago I met Donald. He was fifty-five years old, retired, and very dedicated to meditation. He had been an insurance salesman and an entrepreneur who took pride in what he called "creative financing." He was also adept at real estate and owned several properties. He was wealthy and felt that now he could afford to live without worries.

He came to our meditations and complimented my work profusely. He let me know that he had two students and was teaching meditation at his house. He felt he had accomplished a higher spiritual development through his "unwavering dedication to silence." Donald had been meditating for many years, and had acquired excellent techniques. He dedicated at least four hours a day to sitting in meditation and he felt he was now living a "true spiritual life."

He shared with me, "I have read J. Krishnamurti, and I follow pretty much on his teachings." He spoke softly and his demeanor was gentle. During our conversations he would say, "I have truly worked out my attachments." On the other hand he would say laughingly, "I enjoy food and my little sports car … you can't take that from me!" This seemed contradictory to his statement, his belief, in having "worked out" his attachments. He was obviously attached to his car and to food; he was quite overweight. Furthermore, it was a contradiction to the teachings he said he followed, which strongly emphasize the need to let go of all attachments.

His contradiction, the division within himself, became more clear in a group dialogue in which Donald was one of the participants. During our conversation the subject of finances for survival in our society was brought up. Donald spoke of creative financing, using different schemes to obtain the object of desire, and meditating on abundance. "When I want something I meditate on it. I don't worry about finances. Everything is one, everything is possible. It is like magic," he said. "Me too!" said another member of the group. "I visualize what I want, and get it" was the main consensus. Different visualization methods, dreams, fantasies, and prayers were shared by members of the group, with enthusiastic "Amen!" attitudes. It was like an old church revival, complete with testimonials.

After a lengthy dialogue we were able to see clearly that there were many opinions and beliefs about spirituality, the use of meditation for financial gains, and true mysticism. For some members of the group it was more like the old conflict between spirituality and materialism, which they believed do not mix. Others felt that spirituality "should not" be separate from business or from materialism, and that they were in conflict themselves and were "seeking to unite the two." Still others felt that in true spiritual living, "wealth or poverty are not an issue. If you are rich, you share more. If you are poor, you share what you can."

Donald contended that business and spirituality were two separate things. In business you follow the rules of the established unwritten laws of self-interest. "You see, meditation is one thing, finance is another. I have managed to keep them separate," he said. "In business you can't give ..."

"You said that anyone can use meditation to be abundant; is that not self-interest?" was my response. "Yes, I meditate on abundance myself, but I don't meditate on the financial transactions and details. Money transactions are not always compatible with spirituality, because you have to watch for your investments. You do not understand these things, Ligia, because you are not involved in business."

"If within you these two things are separate and not compatible, you are not in division?" I asked, adding, "Please remember, that in oneness there is no division. You yourself have quoted Krishnamurti on the conflict and fallacies of 'division within the mind' many times."

"Well ... Everything is one, of course, but ..." He stopped and began to ponder.

Later he confessed to another member of the group that his meditations had been disturbed by the deeper inquiries in our group dialogues. Donald did not return to our meditations or dialogues, so I do not know the outcome of his process.

I have met many people around the world with the same opinions and beliefs as Donald. While talking about the importance of oneness, they live in the separation. Their spirituality seems to be an elaboration of the imagination, the fantasies of the New Age belief systems dedicated to the "me." From health to riches, meditation is used for personal gain. People imagine or fantasize themselves as they would like to be and then "go for it," without observing their divided way of thinking, or their denial of any conflict.

When spirituality is based on fantasy, conditioned belief

systems, we do not experience total equanimity. There is always some kind of conflict lurking in our consciousness, and our meditations may be easily disturbed when confronted by deep inquiry into *truth*. Wealthy people are often more concerned with further accumulation of wealth; they do not share very much of what they have, and they care little about serving others unless there is some self-compensation. The poor often live in the preoccupation of becoming wealthy, using the imagination techniques of our learned New Age spirituality. They are then not concerned with serving others in the community, unless there is some kind of "pay-off."

When spirituality is based on a true mystical experience, we are free of divisions and conflict. The meditation practice deepens when we are confronted with profound inquiry into truth. Then there is no reason to be preoccupied with accumulation of material things, or attachment to them. There is no self-centered movement of consciousness; therefore the "me" does not come first, nor is it neglected. There is no separation between materialism and spirituality. If wealthy, we naturally share our wealth in the spirit of love, and joyfully serve others. If poor, we share what we can, and joyfully serve others.

Organized religion has been one of our obvious expressions of spirituality. True organized religions blossom from the true experience of God, brotherhood, compassion, and love in human beings, which is reflected in their principles. When religion is deeply felt, the principles, precepts, or commandments are a daily living action. But when religion is a learned-by-rote process, and there is dissension, corruption, and wars, all the principles, precepts, and commandments are only mind-representations—*just fantasies!*

> *What does spirit mean to you?*
> *How do you experience your spirituality?*

Transitions

Human beings go through periods of transition in different ways. The most common is that of the "mid-life crisis," a rather superficial transition where many people try very hard to maintain their youth. They tint their gray hair, dress to the fashion of the day (whether or not it is appropriate), and sometimes engage in sexual relationships with younger partners, which usually brings about suffering. The fantasy is to stay young and postpone looking old. People going through a superficial change continue to operate in the self-centered, conditioned consciousness of humanity. Therefore they continue to suffer from their attachments to fantasies, their ambitions, and their being stuck in the pleasure/pain cycle.

A different kind of transition is that of Lora D. She is a middle-aged lady who had been rather successful in her life. She had owned two lucrative businesses that both ended, due to the deterioration of the relationship between her and her partners. In between these endeavors she had involved herself for four years in meditation and in New Age spirituality workshops (the kind that advocate money abundance and full self-expression). She said that she had become "very adept at spiritual experiences of oneness," that her "spirit soared," and that at times she felt "there was nothing she could not do." She had used many of the techniques she had learned and applied them in the teachings she offered through her second business venture. She and her partner were doing workshops on how to be organized, have harmony in work relationships, and be successful in business utilizing visualization and spiritual rituals. They were doing very well until something went amiss in their relationship and they ended the partnership.

Lora had been extremely happy in the past and she could not understand why now she was so despondent. It was as though the spiritual life was gone. She could not regain the oneness she once felt, and all her prayers and meditations were in vain. Now at forty-nine years of age, she found herself totally impoverished and depressed, with occasional thoughts of committing suicide.

Lora believed that her "spiritual soaring" and her "oneness" were true spiritual experiences, when in fact (she later discovered) they were *mind facsimiles* (ego-fabricated imitations) of mystical events, a part of the new fantasy created by a New Age movement that has left many people depressed and lonely. Now she wanted to know how to get back to her happy, "spiritual" days.

Through our dialogues Lora began to unveil the meaning of her spirituality. She could see that she depended on her visualization, her prayers, and her rituals to bring the miracles she *believed* were around the corner. She said, "I had so many miracles in my life before, when I was really focused on my spirituality. Now, no matter how much I try, I seem to get off focus." She was rather self-deprecating, so I reminded her that she certainly was being rather harsh with herself, and that being spiritual is being compassionate.

A deeper inquiry brought about the difference between her true experience of spirit and her belief in spirituality as she had learned it from teachers. Her techniques and rituals, she realized, were all self-serving. Many of her dreams had come true, but they did not last. What she had actually learned, she realized, was that you have to work very hard to make your dreams or fantasies come true. Her new techniques, rituals, and prayers were no more than the old conditioning of how to become successful, but with a new twist called "spirituality." "God wants you to be successful and abundant, so go for it!" had been her motto. This was the same motto as that of the prominent teacher she had studied with very intensely; so I suggested that she inquire more deeply into the parallels between the teacher and herself.

Both had been very successful. The teacher, a religious leader, had a big following through television. She taught that through the power of God you could obtain nurturing relationships, abundance, fulfillment, and so on. This teacher had somehow ended in bankruptcy. Lora had been teaching people to be successful in business by calling upon the power of spirit to realize their dreams, become prosperous, and have great working relationships in their lives. She, too, became financially devastated.

The preacher taught through religion; Lora taught through her knowledge of business. They both invoked the power of God for the purpose of fulfilling dreams, fantasies. After a deep inquiry Lora became very clear that this was a self-centered movement of consciousness. Her spirituality was dedicated to the "me," rather than to truly serving other human beings. She had begun to realize that in her "heart of hearts" (her words) she wanted to do more for others than for herself; self-centeredness was not in harmony with her own presently unfolding integrity of heart. "I have a lot to learn about my own process," she admitted. She could see that her great success in teaching abundance ended in suffering because she lacked the true compassion and clarity that allows people to really experience harmonious, nurturing relationships. "I *thought* I was compassionate, but I have a lot of resentment towards my partner," she confessed. With a half-smile she continued, "Not very spiritual, am I?" Some deep-seated pattern broke at that moment, and she exploded in a healthy laugh. These realizations were very freeing for her. "What a fantasy trip I have been on!" she said.

Lora had actually begun to unfold and be free of her conditioned fantasies but was not *fully aware* of her own unfolding. Her old beliefs kept getting in the way of her new clarity. The truth was that she no longer had the old ambitions or fantasies. She was actually moving into a new dimension of consciousness and she felt confused.

Confusion is not uncommon among people who are going through radical psychic changes. For them to see what is truly going on, they usually need someone else to reflect it as a clear mirror.

Transition may be experienced as disruptive of the usual belief systems, traditions, and fantasies. The person in transition seems to go through a period of confusion, loneliness, a sense of loss and *being lost*, not knowing what to do next. Some people call this an identity crisis because they say that they do not know who they really are. They are not like their old selves; they have changed so much that they have hardly anything in common with their families and friends.

It is interesting to observe how old fantasies disappear when people are going through a transition such as Lora's. It is harder for them to imagine a future with any certainty because they live more in the present. The struggle, at least for some people, seems to be in the lack of awareness of their unfolding process in consciousness. They think something is wrong because they no longer have the same feelings, ambitions, or ideas they used to have. I call this mature unfolding. It is tantamount to the transformation people go through in puberty. It is a radical change in body/mind/spirit, often experienced with some confusion.

There are some people in transition who react very differently from Lora, because their change is more superficial. Usually they begin taking all kinds of workshops on art, dancing, acting, music, healing practices, massage, or shamanic healing. They spend a lot of money on their training, imagining themselves becoming artists, actors, or teachers in the new healing circles that practise the laying on of hands, massage, or shamanism. They begin a new set of fantasies about their "new self." It is my observation that what they experience as transition is actually more of a superficial change, a reaction to growing older. The process of a mature or spiritual unfolding seems to be minimal, because they actually exchange an old fantasy for a new one. Sometimes it is a resurgence of a childhood fantasy.

By *mature or spiritual unfolding* I mean that the person in transition is going through a radical shift in his or her entire being— *spiritupsychophysicalness*. The experience is that of a different dimension of consciousness where the person is propelled from a self-centered movement that considers the "me" first, to a true caring for others and the planet. People in this transition are often moved to service. They dedicate more of their time to volunteer work without expectation of recognition, and they do not suffer from attachment to pleasures or material things.

Spiritual experiences are also referred to as mystical experiences or events concerning the nature of our existence. It is difficult to speak about spirit, because these experiences are subjective, relating to one's own personal existence and the universe. For some people, what they believe to be spiritual experiences turn out to be no more than eventually disappointing fantasies. Others experience true mystical events with great beneficial consequences for the recipient as well as for the consciousness of the whole.

Any reference to spirit is, of necessity, just an individual's representation in mind. No two experiences, compared, will be exactly alike. To the experiencer, the spiritual imagery of the experiences is real, not fantasy; but according to our exposition throughout this book, images are representations—fantasies. And as we have seen, these are in the realm of thought, and they may be ruinous, creative, or constructive.

I would like to differentiate between the *nature* and the *content* of spiritual experience. The *nature* of spiritual experience is unique to the psychophysical structure of human beings. The event may be a predominantly auditory perception, a vision, a strong sense, a feeling, or a strong insight or intuition. While the emphasis may differ from individual to individual, the nature of it remains psychophysical. These occurrences are usually considered paranormal experiences, or out of the ordinary. However, given the multitude of experiences humans have reported from time immemorial, they do not seem rare.

The *content* of the spiritual experience depends on the individual's conditioned mind. Thus, according to their particular belief system or their knowledge, people may have a vision of the Buddha, the Christ, the Virgin Mary, a saint, angels, a ghost, or some other kind of apparition. The content of these experiences changes with the times, according to the current, popular content of consciousness of humanity. At present, the experiences of angels and ghosts are in resurgence and are topics for books and television programs. Angel paintings and other angel paraphernalia (earrings, pins, statues, etc.) are gaining popularity.

The nature of spiritual or mystical experience is perhaps more important to investigate than the content, because the nature of the experience is an inherent predisposition based on the psychophysical structure, which is *the same for all human beings*.

The content is the woven fabric of conditioning through

which the experience is interpreted, and may vary drastically between individuals. A deep investigation of the content may provide an understanding of the relationship between different religious beliefs or conditionings, but will not provide a deep understanding of our own true nature as spiritupsychophysical beings.

> *Would you investigate directly, through yourself, the nature and the content of the spiritual experience, the nature of your own existence? Remember, you are your own authority!*

Some people feel that they have never had a spiritual experience and therefore they could not embark on an investigation of an unknown. The challenge here would be to find out if these people expect a spiritual experience to be the kind of event they have read about or learned of through some religion. Not finding anything similar in their own experiences in life, they feel they must not be very spiritual. Sean, an eighty-year-old gentleman, once complained to me that he had never had spiritual experiences and that he was doubtful of his own spirituality. He compared himself to the people in the ashram (a religious community) in which he had lived for several years. "They seem to be able to attain some kind of spiritual highs, but I do not." By constantly measuring himself against others and comparing his experiences to theirs, he kept missing the fact that he was actually living the nature of his existence. He felt whole and was often exalted by wonderful meditations and by his life of service to others. He felt grateful for his life in the universe. Sean lives his spiritual experience without naming it. It just happens not to look like anyone else's!

I am reminded of the experience that astronaut Edgar Mitchell relates. In an interview he commented that while in space, away from the earth, "I had a powerful inner or subjective experience, or you can say a peak experience, or someone will say a mystical experience; and I was trained in the heart of science as firmly as anyone; and immediately I had to come to terms with this. What is it that happened? Why this overwhelming feeling of intelligence, or someone may say a divine presence in the universe; and how and why did that happen? And I was not satisfied with our traditional explanations …"

My interpretation of Edgar Mitchell's experience is that he had the opportunity to truly experience existence through a spiritual or mystical event. Since he did not use any traditional knowledge or beliefs to interpret this event, he was left with a sense of awe and deep questioning. He consequently founded an organization called the Institute of Noetic Sciences, with the purpose of furthering research into consciousness.

Mystical or spiritual experiences often come uninvited, when you least expect them. They are *clear full awareness*. They are not fantasy, an elaboration of conditioned belief systems. In other words, while mystical experiences are representations in the mind of the individual, they are not fantasies originating in the personal memory banks of the experiencer. Mystical events are very real yet inexplicable. Humans have reported them for millennia but have generally assigned them explanations derived from religious beliefs. We do know that they are very powerful subjective experiences and that they usually shift the dimension of consciousness of the person, bringing the thinking process to a different paradigm. As a matter of fact, they seem to produce a radical change in the whole being.

The truth is that we know very little about the nature of mystical or spiritual experiences. We need to inquire further within ourselves and be able to distinguish between fantasy and the true spiritual or mystical event, *full awareness*.

Unfortunately, we live the images of our thinking process and miss the truth of our existence.

Have you heard the saying, "We live mostly in our heads"? Well … the truth is yes, of course we do! While this statement might not be provable through any science, it is discoverable at an experiential level. We live the fantasies that are automatically repeated in our brains as old broken records, without questioning our way of functioning.

Full awareness is transformational, a different realm, a different dimension of consciousness. It is the transcendence of our ordinary conditioned and fantasy-ridden consciousness.

Through these writings we have been observing the power of the thought process, how fantasy—imagination—can affect us in deleterious or beneficial ways. We have differentiated between the destructive and constructive fantasy worlds of our civilization. Through this inquiry it is possible to see the need for a radical change in the consciousness of humanity. I do not mean a superficial change in the way we think (trading old fantasies for new ones) but a fundamental change in *spiritu-psychophysicalness*.

This radical or fundamental change may be more like a transubstantiation needed for the whole planet to survive. This is not something to be achieved by trying to improve ourselves, as is popularly believed. We have been trying to improve for thousands of years; still we continue to submerge ourselves further in the mire of our own fantasies, our conditioning.

We need to confront, without judgment or evaluation, the truth of our own functioning, and thus allow our own wisdom, our natural intelligence, the energy that is creation itself, to unfold.

To that end our greatest blessing is in the power of full awareness, which is a gift of creation.

15.

Spiritupsychophysicalness

The quest for truth, wholeness, and true love seems to be an eternal natural movement in our consciousness. In this quest, through observation and inquiry into wholeness, I came to an experience of our true nature, *spiritupsychophysicalness*.[1]

As explained in the Preamble of this book, there are no dashes in the word to separate the aspects of spirit, psyche, and physicalness. Using a single word helps evoke the truth of our totality, at least in our conceptual understanding of ourselves without fantasy, and perhaps open doors to the true experience of our wholeness.

Traditionally, we have separated the three basic discernible aspects of humanness into spirit, mind (or psyche), and body. We have done this through our natural sensorial experience as well as through our concepts and beliefs. Thus we came to feel and believe that we are these three distinct separate parts— spirit, body, and mind.

We have seen throughout this book that the activity of the body/mind is inseparable. Nonetheless, the thinking process *disunites* that which is whole (the universe); it *separates* things into parts (from celestial bodies to ourselves as organisms); and

---

[1] This chapter was originally published as an article in *The Quest* magazine (Theosophical Society in America, Winter, 1994). Some of the text has been adapted for this book.

it further *fragments* the parts (as the divisions we feel within ourselves).

Perhaps this traditional, disuniting way of thinking is related to our natural way of functioning. It may have been primarily influenced by our own senses, which give us a perception of total separateness. That is, our eyes, skin, nose, ears, and tongue give us the sensation of an outer reality that is separate from the inner reality of the sensation itself. Let us say we touch something warm with our hand; the feeling or sensation (the electrical impulses, etc.) localized within the body, per se, is one reality; at the same time we get the distinct feeling of the mass and temperature of the object we touched as something beyond our hand's skin, a separate reality. Thus we experience ourselves as separate bodies. As my friend Robert Tompkins, Professor at Western Oregon State College, remarks, "Even at the level of the immune system, cells distinguish one's own body from foreign organisms. Separateness seems essential to life."

Physically, separateness is directly related to survival, and psychically, through our thought process, we elaborate ways to protect and provide for our survival. This experience of separation has given rise to an image of ourselves—"I," "me"—as well as images of others—"he," "she," "they."

It is feasible that our old beliefs in the separation of body and mind come from the way we sense thinking, mind, and emotions, as well as more subtle psychological feelings.

For example, we feel someone's insult as a psychological attack (mental cruelty) and not as a physical attack. This is a definite separation in our interpretation (our thinking) even though we experience the emotion in our bodies.

If our thinking is based on our perception of separateness, then it follows that the thinking paradigms we develop will be separative; and indeed this is reflected in our scientific theories, philosophies, and religions. To the great majority of people in this world, spirit, mind, and body still are experienced as three different parts of the "me," as entities living together and managed by external and internal forces.

Furthermore, it may be assumed that our tendency to generalize the thinking process, through multiple linear associations, is responsible for the beliefs in the separation of everything on the planet and in the universe, including a separate soul or spirit, and a separate God.

The natural physical sensation of separateness may tacitly and unconsciously be a constant influence on our way of thinking. Despite present knowledge in physics of the interconnectedness in the universe, and despite religious and philosophical beliefs in Oneness, we generally do not, in our daily living, truly experience ourselves as being One. We do not experience *spiritupsychophysicalness*.

Looking at the general predicament of the planet and the behavior of human beings at large tells us that humanity is very far from behavior that manifests a true experience of Oneness, which is the experience of true brotherhood or love.

Thinking is an intrinsic function of the human organism and, through millennia, it has developed different paradigms. We inherit, or rather learn, a particular way of thinking through acculturation. Thus each society or culture passes on, from generation to generation, beliefs developed through conditioned thinking processes, which are maintained in the memory banks of humanity.

Let us assume that our disuniting and fragmentary way of thinking is indeed a natural occurrence. Furthermore, let us say that this is due to our own way of functioning as human organisms, which is accentuated by our conditioning. This brings some questions to mind. Is it possible to actually experience our wholeness while, simultaneously, feeling divided by our own sensorial way of functioning and way of thinking? Is there a way of knowing beyond the thinking process? If so, is it imperative that we transcend fragmentary thinking to experience directly our totality—that is, spiritupsychophysicalness? In the words of Lao Tsu,

> Carrying body and soul and embracing the one
> Can you avoid separation?

Looking at the term spiritupsychophysicalness may bring the

idea that we are trying to unify the three aspects of spirit, body, and mind. I suggest that this is an impossibility, for paradoxically, unbeknownst to us, within our deepest experience of our humanness, we already possess a natural "knowing" that we have never been separate. Thus, the ancient Sage could speak directly from personal experience of the oneness of the universe.

> Look, it cannot be seen—it is beyond form.
> Listen, it cannot be heard—it is beyond sound.
> Grasp, it cannot be held—it is intangible.
> These three are indefinable;
> Therefore they are joined in one.
>
> From above it is not bright;
> From below it is not dark:
> An unbroken thread beyond description.
> It returns to nothingness.
> The form of the formless,
> The image of the imageless,
> It is called indefinable and beyond imagination.
>
> Stand before it and there is no beginning.
> Follow it and there is no end.
> Stay with the ancient Tao,
> Move with the present.
>
> Knowing the ancient beginning is the essence of the TAO.
> —Lao Tsu

The ancient sages based their teachings on their intuitive power rather than on the established knowledge of their time. They were wise human beings who could see beyond the conditioned way of thinking of their societies. Perhaps they are the proof that there is an awareness (intuition or insight) available to human beings that is beyond ordinary conditioned thought. All sages are peaceful human beings who are able to point to truth, to wholeness, while being living examples of their teachings. They are not bound to repeating written teachings or dogma while living contrary to their words.

It is important to differentiate between the wisdom of the sages and the prevalent disuniting, separating, and fragmentary paradigms of thinking typical of our present humanity. Any human being can be intuitive. However, this wonderful quality is stifled by the need to acculturate (to be conditioned to society in order to survive). Thus we learn to think in terms of our culture's paradigms of thought.

The self-centered consciousness of the "me" is the most prevalent paradigm of thinking in humanity as a whole. This is an unaware and fragmentary way of thinking in which this "me" is generalized to "my country," "my religion," "my property," etc. Preoccupation with the "me" excludes wholeness and consideration for others (except in relationship to the "me"). The present state of our planet, with its overpopulation, starvation, pollution, and wars, attests to this.

This paradigm of thinking, revolving around individualistic concerns, prevents our freedom to experience our true holistic nature directly through insight or intuition. In other words, our current way of thinking lacks true awareness or wisdom.

To *analyze* or *teach* spiritupsychophysicalness would be to repeat a pattern that is within our present paradigm of thinking—learn and repeat—and would not allow individuals the deep *experience* of truth. We consider intellectual knowledge more important than experiential knowing. To repeat this pattern would be an insult to the natural wisdom of the reader. Therefore, we have actually been looking at some of the important barriers to the direct experience of our wholeness. It will be entirely up to you to continue to explore other barriers to the experience of your true nature, and that of humanity at large.

It is the intent of these writings to point to the way we function as human beings, without reference to any particular philosophy, science, psychological theory, or religious belief. They do not propound a new theory or aspire to design a new way of thinking. Rather, this is a proposal for an investigation into consciousness, the possible results of our own way of functioning, and the true nature of being human—what I called spiritupsychophysicalness.

Since this word is a neologism it is not associated with any traditional way of thinking. There is no need to compare it with anything known, nor is it necessary to believe or disbelieve in the term itself. It would be ludicrous to try to convince you or to sell you a technique to experience that which is in your own power to discover. I am not offering another fantasy.

> *You are encouraged to look anew without the*
> *assistance of knowledge, to look without judging*
> *or evaluating. To do this is to look in a*
> *meditative way, thus allowing your own wisdom*
> *to unfold the truth from a kind of silence.*

The following is my indulgent sharing of the experience of spiritupsychophysicalness. IT IS NOT A TEACHING.

Spirit is Space. It is my observation that everything is manifested in Space; all heavenly bodies are created in what we perceive as Space. We exist on a planet which is the creation of the energy's organizing principles in Space. Human forms are also aggregates of that same energy's organizing principles.

I have referred to space as Spirit, or the creating force of every*thing*. I propose that Spirit, or Space, or Organizing Energies may be experienced, with or without traditional dogma, as God.

Spirit or Space is the unmanifest/manifest and basic aspect of our totality; thus the beginning of the word spiritupsychophysicalness—*spiritu*—carries this experience of Space or God or Spirit as an intrinsic manifestation in matter/energy.

The middle part of the word—*psychophysical*—carries the experience of the nature of our existence, the aggregate of energy into atoms and molecules, and manifested into body/mind, where everything is experienced and expressed.

The most important clue is the suffix *ness*, which, according to the dictionary, means state or quality—or instance of being. One could say that the organizing principles of Space into life forms are manifested in our planet from the single cell organisms to complex animals, plants, and humankind.

The impermanence of these aggregates of energy points to

the fact that life is a *state of being* within a planet, constantly changing in a universe created by *Space—Spirit—God*. The impermanence of our body/mind or psychophysicalness is therefore a particular state of being or energy, which we know as existence.

I chose the suffix *ness* to represent *our state of beingness*, thus completing in word form the whole meaning of the experience.

In the true experience of spiritupsychophysicalness, there is no separation between spiritual, physical, and mental, nor is there an alteration in our sense perception of separateness, for we continue to function as psychophysical beings just the same. We continue to function in representations of mind.

Thus, the paradoxical truth is, in Oneness there is separation.

ALL is SPACE, ALL is SPIRIT, ALL is MATTER, ALL is MENTAL, ALL is ENERGY, ALL is GOD. In this experience, there is gratefulness for the awareness of the blessings of existence, without denying the lack of awareness and the suffering in humanity.

ALL is respected equally, for the Holomovement of Universe is *ALL there is*. Therefore, no feelings of inward divisions, no "me," no divisions between humans, plants, animals, earth, seas, or celestial bodies, regardless of sense perceptions of separation.

The quest for truth is a perennial psychophysical activity in humanity. The opportunity for the experience of truth is spiritually ever-present in the mystery beyond our own fantasies, conditioning, and way of functioning.

The experience of spiritupsychophysicalness is a transcendence of conditioned thinking—an experience of true love. When the spiritual or mystical experience of love is manifested in our daily conduct, then the experience is no longer just a representation—fantasy—but a living action.

We are states of being, *we are love, existence in its totality*. This, my friends, we can experience deeply and directly, through our own wisdom, in *this living moment of eternity.*

Index